D1612429

China and Angola

A Marriage of Convenience?

Through the voices of the peoples of Africa and the global South, Pambazuka Press and Pambazuka News disseminate analysis and debate on the struggle for freedom and justice.

Pambazuka Press – www.pambazukapress.org

A Pan-African publisher of progressive books and DVDs on Africa and the global South that aim to stimulate discussion, analysis and engagement. Our publications address issues of human rights, social justice, advocacy, the politics of aid, development and international finance, women's rights, emerging powers and activism. They are primarily written by well-known African academics and activists. Most books are also available as ebooks.

Pambazuka News – www.pambazuka.org

The award-winning and influential electronic weekly newsletter providing a platform for progressive Pan-African perspectives on politics, development and global affairs. With more than 2,800 contributors across the continent and a readership of more than 660,000, Pambazuka News has become the indispensable source of authentic voices of Africa's social analysts and activists.

Pambazuka Press and Pambazuka News are published by Fahamu (www.fahamu.org)

China and Angola

A Marriage of Convenience?

Edited by Marcus Power
and Ana Cristina Alves

Pambazuka Press
An imprint of Fahamu

Published 2012 by Pambazuka Press, an imprint of Fahamu
Cape Town, Dakar, Nairobi and Oxford
www.pambazukapress.org www.fahamu.org www.pambazuka.org

Fahamu Kenya, PO Box 47158, 00100 GPO, Nairobi, Kenya
Fahamu Senegal, 9 Cité Sonatel 2, BP 13083 Dakar Grand-Yoff,
Dakar, Senegal
Fahamu South Africa, c/o 19 Nerina Crescent, Fish Hoek,
7975 Cape Town, South Africa
Fahamu UK, 2nd floor, 51 Cornmarket Street, Oxford OX1 3HA, UK

British Library Cataloguing in Publication Data
A catalogue record for this book is available from the British Library

ISBN: 978-0-85749-107-7 paperback
ISBN: 978-0-85749-108-4 ebook – pdf
ISBN: 978-0-85749-109-1 ebook – epub
ISBN: 978-0-85749-110-7 ebook – Kindle

Manufactured on demand by Lightning Source

Contents

Contributors

Chris Alden is reader in the international relations department at the London School of Economics and head of the Global Powers in Africa programme at the South African Institute of International Affairs (SAIIA)

Ana Cristina Alves is senior researcher with the Global Powers in Africa programme at the South African Institute of International Affairs (SAIIA) and assistant professor at the Institute of Social and Political Sciences, Technical University of Lisbon.

Lucy Corkin is a research associate at the Africa–Asia Centre at SOAS, University of London

Sylvia Croese is a PhD candidate at the African doctoral academy of Stellenbosch University.

Sofia Fernandes is a PhD candidate at ISCTE, Lisbon University Institute and researcher at the Centre for African Studies, ISCTE-IUL.

Liu Haifang is an associate professor in the school of international studies and deputy director, secretary general of the centre for African studies at Peking University.

Assis Malaquias is professor and chair, defense economics, Africa Center for Strategic Studies, National Defense University, Washington, DC.

Marcus Power is a professor of human geography in the department of geography at the University of Durham and co-author of *China's Resource Diplomacy in Africa: Powering Development?*

Amália Quintão is an economist, senior researcher and lecturer at the centre for studies and scientific research (CEIC) at the Catholic University of Angola (UCAN), and director of the audit office at ENSA (Angolan Public Insurance Enterprise).

Regina Santos is an economist and researcher at the centre for studies and scientific research (CEIC) at the Catholic University of Angola (UCAN). She is part of the research team that works on Angola's yearly economic and social reports.

Alex Vines, OBE, is research director for area studies and international law and head of the Africa Programme at Chatham House.

Markus Weimer is research fellow at the Africa Programme and coordinator of the Angola forum at Chatham House.

Introduction: China and Angola's partnership

Marcus Power and Ana Cristina Alves

Despite the considerable escalation of cooperation between China and Angola in recent years and the explosion of media and academic interest in China's broader engagement with Africa, the precise terms of this emerging partnership and its practical implications have remained rather unclear. Researching the changing dynamics of China–Angola relations is therefore far from straightforward and there are a number of important reasons for this. One of the most significant is the lack of transparency (in both China and Angola) about the precise terms of the development assistance, trade and investment flows between the two countries. Until relatively recently there were few if any official statements of the exact amount of Chinese lending to Angola[1] and despite the growing international momentum around the effectiveness of aid, historically China has been reticent to reveal and talk about its 'aid' contributions in Africa (Tan-Mullins et al 2010) although this is slowly beginning to change (Grimm 2011). On the Angolan side one need only look at the scandal following the IMF's revelation[2] in December 2011 that $32 billion in government funds were spent or transferred from 2007 to 2010 without being properly documented in the budget[3] (IMF 2011) a sum equivalent to one quarter of the country's gross domestic product (GDP). The scandal originated from the state oil firm, Sonangol, now dubbed the 'quasi-fiscal operations manager' of the Angolan government. In December 2011 Human Rights Watch urged the government to provide a full public accounting for the missing government funds (Human Rights Watch 2011) and a month later the Angolan news agency, Angop, cited a statement from the government saying that it denied the funds were missing and that the government admitted there was a discrepancy in accounts but believed this was a result of 'insufficient records' (Reuters 2012). There are also the rather 'tangled webs' that characterise China–Angola business relations, particularly those that surround the loans to Angola from the China

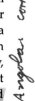

Angolan corruption (handwritten margin note)

1

International Fund (CIF) centred upon the Queensway group in Hong Kong (Levkowitz et al 2009) or those involved in the establishment of China Sonangol International Holding (CSIH),[4] a joint venture set up in 2004 between Sonangol and Hong Kong-based private business interests (Vines et al 2009). Some of the agencies set up to manage Chinese loans in Angola, such as the Gabinete de Reconstrução Nacional (GRN),[5] have also demonstrated a real lack of transparency.

The growing importance of Chinese credit lines and the increasing presence of Chinese corporate agencies across Angolan territory raise important questions about development, poverty reduction and inequality, about governance and labour relations and about Angola's institutional capacity and the social structure of its cities (Power 2011). The intensification of this partnership also raises important policy challenges, especially in Angola where the role of Chinese loans and investment has been critical to the country's post-conflict reconstruction. In organising a major international conference in Luanda in January 2011 to explore and discuss these challenges (as well as the possible policy responses to them) we felt that there was a pressing need to assess the implications of Chinese economic assistance, trade and investment for Angolan development and to create a space in which these implications could be debated publicly. We also felt there were a significant number of myths and misconceptions surrounding the current terms of China–Angola cooperation that we wanted to debunk. The idea for organising this event first took shape in a informal meeting attended by Giles Mohan, Marcus Power, Alex Vines, Chris Alden and Ana Alves at the London School of Economics in late 2009 and was partly conceived as a follow-up to the first conference on China–Angola relations held at the Centro de Estudos e Investigação Científica (CEIC) of the Catholic University of Angola (UCAN).

The venue for the conference in Luanda was the Hotel Skyna in Avenida de Portugal and the event itself was jointly organised by the University of Durham, CEIC at UCAN and the South African Institute of International Affairs (SAIIA) with support from the UK Department for International Development (DfID), the UK's Economic and Social Research Council (ESRC),[6] the University of Durham, SAIIA and the African Economic Research Consortium

(AERC). The conference objectives were: (1) to assist policy makers in Angola in understanding the opportunities and challenges of Chinese engagement for planning national development and post-war reconstruction strategies; (2) to facilitate and intensify a public dialogue between Chinese officials and companies operating in Angola and Angolan governmental/non-governmental agencies on the terms of partnership and the potential and limits of cooperation; (3) to assist Angolan NGOs, regional organisations and international donors in developing their capacity to understand and interpret the impact of Chinese intervention and partnership in Angola and (4) to increase awareness and understanding of the implications of China's engagement with Angolan development and to enhance the capacity of Angolan research institutions by promoting greater international academic collaboration around the study of international partnerships in Angola. By creating a dialogue between the research community investigating China–Angola relations and end users of the research, the conference thus sought to bring key stakeholders together so that evidence-based research could begin to influence policy and practice.

In promoting greater international academic collaboration around the study of international partnerships in Angola, the conference involved a gathering of scholars working in Angola, China, Portugal, South Africa, the US, and the UK. The nine chapters of this book are based on contributions from the conference,[7] many of which draw directly upon primary fieldwork conducted by the contributors in Angola and China. Although the clear focus of the event was on Angola's relations with China, some of the contributions draw on examples from elsewhere on the continent and many recognised that a number of other established and emerging international powers are currently attempting to engage Angola as a strategic partner, following greater international recognition of the country's oil wealth. Angola continues to actively pursue a strategy of diversification of its international political and economic relationships (Vines et al 2009) and has sought to expand the range of its bilateral and commercial relations by negotiating deals and credit lines with a range of other 'partners', including Belgium, Brazil, Canada, Germany, India, Israel, Italy, France, Japan, Portugal, South Korea Spain, the UK, the US and the European Union.[8] Thus some of the contributors situated their analysis of China–Angola relations within the context of the broader range of international partnerships that Angola has been developing in recent years or explored the reaction among Western donors to these new partnerships for 'development'. In this respect China is not the only show in town and Chinese engagement with Angola needs to be understood in the geopolitical context of the wider contemporary 'scramble for Africa' of which it is a part (Power and Mohan 2010).

The conference was extremely well attended and over 140 delegates were present on the day. In addition to a wide range of Angolan and foreign scholars working on China–Angola relations the event was attended by high-level officials from several interested Angolan government institutions that are directly involved in the China–Angola partnership. These included the vice minister of petroleum, the former spokesman of the cabinet (currently heading the National Private Investment Agency – ANIP), the secretary of state for cooperation of the ministry of external affairs, and senior officials from the ministries of finance, external affairs, commerce, urban planning and construction and petroleum. Conference participants also included representatives of Angolan NGOs including Development Workshop, Open Society Angola and Acção para o Desenvolvimento Rural e Ambiente (ADRA). UK Foreign and Commonwealth Office (FCO) officials in Luanda attended the conference along with UK Ambassador Richard Wildash (who kindly hosted a post-conference reception at the embassy for all conference delegates), the Chinese ambassador to Angola, Zhang Bolun, along with the ambassadors of Norway, Portugal and South Africa. The general tone of interventions by Angolan policy makers and civil society was broadly supportive of China's involvement and contribution to Angolan development. The developmental gains of new infrastructure and the utility of having alternatives to traditional donors were acknowledged by policy makers and civil society alike. Nonetheless, concerns were raised around the lack of transparency in the credit lines and their terms; the quality of the infrastructure being provided; the large numbers of Chinese workers across the country and the social impact of future Chinese involvement in sectors such as agriculture and land.

The conference received extensive media coverage both in Angola and internationally. Some of the presenters contributed

KEY
* CONCERNS

news articles about the event to the media and gave interviews about China–Angola relations to journalists from Angola and beyond including Televisão Pública de Angola (TPA), *Jornal Expansão*, *Jornal de Angola*, Rádio e Televisão de Portugal (RTP), the Inter Press Service (IPS), the BBC and Radio France International. Three Angolan TV stations included coverage of the conference in their news bulletins and the event was also covered by representatives from Angolan radio stations such as Rádio Nacional de Angola and Rádio Ecclésia. The key headlines from the conference were also reported in online news outlets across Africa including news agencies in Guinea-Bissau, Kenya, Mozambique, and South Africa.

The chapters in this book offer a rich overview of China–Angola relations. They not only cover different dimensions of the relationship but also convey a diversity of perceptions regarding the nature of the partnership. Chris Alden sets the broad framework of China–Africa relations. He discusses the key drivers of China's foray into Africa, the wide spectrum of Chinese actors involved and the role of the Forum on China–Africa Cooperation (FOCAC) as a strategic diplomatic forum, emphasising the resilience and versatility of its policies and the changing nature of the relationship.

Assis Malaquias examines the internal synergies throughout the Angolan civil war that provided the rationale for Luanda's multi-pronged foreign policy, and analyses how China fits into this picture, arguing that while Beijing might be a critical ally in helping to fulfil pressing internal challenges it is not regarded by Luanda as a long-term strategic partner.

In the same vein, Lucy Corkin examines the ways in which Angola's political elites have managed Chinese credit lines, arguing that relations with China have formed part of a successful strategy not only to bolster regime stability domestically but also to boost the international standing of the Angolan government. Corkin illustrates how Angola's political elites have used Chinese political and commercial actors to keep internal political rivalries in check and to retain political dominance through a consolidation both of the sources of economic rent and of the discourse of national reconstruction.

Sofia Fernandes provides a historical overview of China–Angola relations and examines Chinese involvement in Angola's energy, construction, retail and wholesale sectors along with some of the labour/employment issues that this has raised. Fernandes argues that this widespread engagement of the Chinese community in a variety of sectors of the Angolan economy (as wholesale traders, in the private construction business, as growers and vendors of fruits and vegetables, as urban and rural traders) are signs that Chinese workers entering the country have been moving away from the status of 'controlled' contract workers on limited-duration projects and are now beginning to settle in Angola.

Markus Weimer and Alex Vines examine how China has been able to access Angolan oil through infrastructure deals during the period 2003–2011, examining the emergence of Sinopec in Angola, the competition and rivalry between Chinese interests and actors in Angola (and between China and other would-be suitors such as India) and the role that the CIF is playing in Angola and other parts of sub-Saharan Africa. Noting that the influence of China in Angola is often overplayed, Weimer and Vines point out that there is a growing sense of fatigue among Angolan officials with the West's 'fixation' with this relationship.

Ana Alves analyses in detail Sinopec's footprint in the Angolan oil industry, offering an insight into the dynamics of its relationship with Sonangol over the past decade. Alves explores the synergies underlying the ebbs and flows of the Sinopec–Sonangol partnership and examines how Sonangol managed to tame Sinopec's ambitions in Angola's upstream oil sector.

Sylvia Croese critically analyses the implementation of Angola's housing policy in the post-war era and the ad hoc, costly, centrally planned and implemented national urbanism and housing programme inspired by the modernist model of development, with its clear emphasis on infrastructure, that the MPLA has followed. Croese examines the involvement of Chinese firms in a range of housing-related reconstruction projects (including the construction of 'social housing') and notes that despite the government's recent proclamations of commitment to transparency and accountability the needs and capacities of Angola's citizens are consistently ignored or overlooked.

Amália Quintão and Regina Santos develop an analysis of Chinese corporate practices in Angola based on a survey of the perceptions of Angolan workers. This empirical study unpacks a variety of myths regarding the impact of Chinese labour practices on the local labour market and argues for the need to put in place a better local regulatory environment so as to tackle the existing shortcomings and foster the benefits stemming from this cultural, economic and professional interchange.

Liu Haifang reviews a range of Chinese-language literatures concerned with Angola (including newspapers, academic journals and popular magazines and journals) and discerns some notable shifts in Chinese perceptions of the country since the early 1980s. Haifang illustrates that some of what has been written in Chinese about the country has been produced by people who had previously worked as practitioners on bilateral cooperation projects or as employees in Chinese engineering and construction projects and demonstrates the importance of the 'everyday' grassroots interactions which have often been overlooked in accounts of China–Angola relations.

We would like to thank all the participants in the workshop for their valuable input, particularly the contributors to this volume for their enthusiasm and commitment. We would also like to express our gratitude to the funders that supported the conference and the publication of this book. We would also like to thank Claire Watkins and Rachel Wiggans for their help with copyediting and Salim Valimamade, Alves da Rocha and Margarida Teixeira at UCAN for all their support and encouragement in planning and organising the conference.

The title of this book is borrowed from a 2011 paper by Lucy Corkin 'China and Angola: Strategic partnership or marriage of convenience?', published by Chr. Michelsen Institute and Centro de Estudos e Investigação Científica.

Notes

1. Ambassador Zhang Bolun said that three state banks – the Export-Import Bank of China, the Industrial and Commercial Bank of China and the China Development Bank – have extended $14.5 billion in credit to Angola since 2002 (RNW 2011). He also noted that more than 50 state-owned companies and 400 private companies are involved in Angola's reconstruction, with 60–70,000 Chinese expatriates residing in the country.
2. In 2009 the Angolan government made a stand-by agreement with the IMF which granted Luanda a loan of $1.4 billion to stabilise its balance

of payments following an abrupt drop in net foreign reserves from the previous year. That pact opened doors for IMF officials to scrutinise Angolan government spending.

3. The lack of transparency in the management of public resources has historically made accountability difficult to achieve and a considerable amount of revenue has disappeared into what has been referred to as the 'Bermuda Triangle' between the state oil company Sonangol, the treasury and the National Bank (Hodges 2004). From 1997 to 2002, unaccounted-for funds from oil revenues amounted to some $4.22 billion (Human Rights Watch 2004). In 2011 Global Witness also found a $8.55 billion difference in the reported figures for oil revenue between Sonangol and the ministries of finance and petroleum (Global Witness 2011:5).

4. There is also Sonangol Sinopec International (SSI), a joint venture between Sinopec and the CSIH which has the backing of key members of the Angolan elite.

5. In 2010 the Angolan President Eduardo dos Santos announced that a company called Sonangol Imobiliária (Sonangol Real Estate) would be taking over responsibility from the GRN for implementing various projects relating to construction and the rehabilitation of infrastructure (*Jornal de Angola* 2010).

6. The ESRC provided support for a research project entitled 'The politics of Chinese engagement with African development: case studies of Angola and Ghana' involving Professor Giles Mohan (Open University), Professor Marcus Power (University of Durham) and Dr May Tan-Mullins (University of Nottingham). The award reference code was RES-062–23-0487.

7. With the exception of the chapter by Assis Malaquias, which was not originally presented at the conference.

8. Interestingly, in November 2011 Angolan President Eduardo dos Santos said that, due to the severity of Portugal's economic and financial crisis and its need for austerity measures and a bail out, Angola was ready to help, while the Angolan government was said to be studying Portugal's privatisation plans 'very deeply' (BBC 2011; *Economist* 2011).

References

BBC (British Broadcasting Corporation) (2011) 'Angola's Eduardo dos Santos offers help to Portugal', 18 November, http://www.bbc.co.uk/news/world-africa-15790127, accessed 1 February 2012

Economist (2011) 'Angola and Portugal: role reversal – an ex-colony may be getting the better, in economic terms, of its old master', 3 September, http://www.economist.com/node/21528310, accessed 1 February 2012

Global Witness (2011) 'Oil revenues in Angola: much more information, but not enough transparency', London, Global Witness

Grimm, S. (2011) 'Transparency of Chinese aid: an analysis of the published information on Chinese external financial flows', http://www.

publishwhatyoufund.org/files/Transparency-of-Chinese-Aid_final.pdf, accessed 1 February 2012

Hodges, A. (2004) *Angola: Anatomy of an Oil State*, Oxford, James Currey

Human Rights Watch (2004) 'Some transparency, no accountability: the use of oil revenue in Angola and its impact on human rights', http://www.hrw.org/en/reports/2004/01/12/some-transparency-no-accountability, accessed 1 February 2012

Human Rights Watch (2011) 'Angola: explain missing government funds – state oil company is main focus of investigation', http://www.hrw.org/news/2011/12/20/angola-explain-missing-government-funds, accessed 1 February 2012

IMF (International Monetary Fund) Angola (2011) 'Fifth review under the stand-by arrangement', 26 October, http://www.imf.org/external/pubs/ft/scr/2011/cr11346.pdf, accessed 1 February 2012

Jornal de Angola (2010) 'Imobiliária da Sonangol gere novas centralidades', 28 September

Levkowitz, L., Ross, M.M. and Warner, J.R. (2009) 'The 88 Queensway Group: a case study in Chinese investors' operations in Angola and beyond', Washington, US–China Economic and Security Review Commission, http://www.uscc.gov/The_88_Queensway_Group.pdf, accessed 12 April 2012

Power, M. and Mohan, G. (2010) 'Towards a critical geopolitics of China's engagement with African development', *Geopolitics* 15: 462–95

Power, M. (2011) 'Angola 2025: the future of the "world's richest poor country" as seen through a Chinese rear-view mirror', Antipode

Reuters (2012) 'Angola denies $32 billion missing in state funds', http://af.reuters.com/article/topNews/idAFJOE80H00Z20120118, accessed 1 February 2012

Radio Netherlands Worldwide (RNW) (2011) 'China lends Angola $15 billion but creates few jobs', 6 March. http://www.rnw.nl/africa/bulletin/china-lends-angola-15-bn-creates-few-jobs, accessed 5 March 2012

Tan-Mullins, M., Mohan, G. and Power, M. (2010) 'Redefining aid in the China–Africa context', *Development and Change*, 41(5): 857–81

Vines, A., Wong, L., Weimer, M. and Campos, I. (2009) *Thirst for African Oil: Asian National Oil Companies in Nigeria and Angola*, London, Chatham House

1

China and Africa: from engagement to partnership

Chris Alden

The rise of China, from being a stalwart of revolution in the 1950s to its emergence as a global economic and political actor in the last decade, is one of the defining features of the 21st century. For the leading industrialised economies of the North, their initial praise of China's gradualist shift to a market economy has evolved into a chorus bemoaning the Chinese impact on their trade competitiveness and growing concern as they are upstaged internationally by Beijing. These developments are most clearly visible in Africa, a once-forgotten continent that had been languishing on the margins of international interest since the ending of the cold war. China's forthright engagement with the African continent, built upon its historical support for the independence struggle and increasingly the economic power wielded by Beijing, has helped re-ignite continental economies through new investment and trade opportunities as well as restore African political agency within the international system.

The sources of Chinese engagement with Africa

Since the onset of economic reform in 1978, China has had an unmatched record of sustained growth that has transformed key sectors of its economy and made it the globe's leading site for manufacturing and production. To keep the high levels of domestic output, seen to be crucial not only for the Chinese economy but for overall social and political stability in this authoritarian state, the economy needs critical energy, mineral and other resources from abroad (Soares de Oliveira 2008: 83–109). The promulgation of the government's 'going out' strategy, whereby ultimately over a hundred restructured state-owned enterprises were given the legal and administrative means, preferential access to finance, and diplomatic support necessary to break into markets outside of China, has been the main policy response to this need. Given the financial resources of what, in the aftermath of the global financial crisis in 2008, had become the world's largest holder of capital, with over $2.4 trillion in foreign reserves, applying these to the problem of carving out a position in the energy and strategic minerals markets was, in retrospect, fairly straightforward in a capital-starved African environment. Concurrently, the willingness of the Chinese government to provide a whole package of inducements alongside any leasing or supply agreements for resources, aimed at elite-defined needs ranging from presidential palaces to large-scale infrastructure projects, has proved to be crucial to securing deals in Africa.[1] Underlying this approach is a highly publicised provision whereby the Chinese government forswears any interest in the domestic affairs of African governments, in direct contrast to the European Union or the United States, both of whom have selectively applied conditions to their development assistance programmes and even to some investments. In parallel with this state-led drive for resources abroad is a search for new markets aimed at expanding the investment and trade opportunities for Chinese firms, though the relatively small size of the African market poses some constraints on Chinese ambitions. And, finally, there is a diplomatic imperative tied to the decades of competition between Beijing and Taipei over official recognition, with countries in Africa being particularly targeted.

Resource security

China's position within Africa's resource sector has surged in the last decade and a half, starting as a marginal player and now holding significant interests in oil leases from Angola to Sudan, and mining concessions from the Democratic Republic of the Congo to South Africa. Its two way trade with Africa, exceeding $160 billion in 2011, is overwhelmingly based on the extraction of oil, strategic minerals and a few raw materials in exchange for manufactured goods (Goldstein et al 2006). Reflecting these trends, China went from leading Asian oil exporter in 1993 to, a few years later, the second largest world consumer (2003) and third global importer (2004). This fact alone justifies the reallocation of energy security to the core of Beijing's foreign policy formulation[2] since, as Zweig and Jianhai point out, not only is China's continued economic growth dependent on securing the supply of resources but so is its social stability and ultimately the survival of the Communist Party of China (CPC).

Despite being among the major oil producers (5.2 per cent share of world's production in 2010)[3] and being second only to the US in refinery capacity (11 per cent and 19.2 per cent respectively),[4] China is only able to provide for less than half of its domestic oil needs.[5] In a broader perspective China accounted for 10.6 per cent of world oil consumption in 2010 (still lagging far behind the world's major oil consumer, the US, 21.1 per cent) and 12.5 per cent of total oil imports (second after the US's 24 per cent share) (BP 2011). China's oil consumption has doubled in the last decade and according to OPEC, China's oil demand will show the world's fastest growth rate in the coming decades, doubling again by 2035 when its demand is expected to be over 18 million barrels per day (bpd) (OPEC 2011: 63).

China became a net oil importer in 1993 but it was not until the new century that energy security became central to the political debate. Although other energy sources (such as coal, natural gas, nuclear energy, hydropower and alternative fuels) are inherent to this debate, oil is the utmost Chinese concern since it represents its largest external reliance. Furthermore, concerns about the growing instability in the Middle East and now North Africa pushed for a diversification strategy which because of the inherent complementarities swiftly placed Africa high in Beijing's new suppliers' list. Uneasiness over this topic among the political elite has continued to grow in recent years, as illustrated by the creation of the Energy Leading Group in 2005, the publication of a White Paper on energy ('China's Energy Conditions and Policies')[6] in December 2007 and the White Paper on diplomacy in July 2008 whose first chapter is on 'The issue of energy security during the period of high oil prices' (Hsiao 2008).

In addition to oil and in order to sustain its economic growth, China also became externally dependent on other sectors of the extraction industry, further justifying its growing economic interaction with the African continent in the new century. Over the past decade China surpassed the US to become the world-leading consumer of most base metals. Chinese demand has been growing at a rate over 10 per cent a year since 1990 having even intensified in recent years (Brett and Ericsson 2006: 22) and is the major driver behind the soaring prices of metals in the international market. China is the world's largest consumer and producer of aluminium, iron ore, lead and zinc and holds significant shares in all other minerals supply-and-demand markets.

Finally, food security itself is becoming an area of great concern for China. The years of rapid economic development have, for the first time in decades, exposed China to vagaries of supply and market constraints in agricultural commodities. In terms of overall agricultural imports, China leads the region with its import share of 44 per cent of the world's soybeans, 35 per cent of the world's cotton, 20 per cent of the world's palm oil and 2.5 per cent of the world's rice, with Japanese, Indian and South Korean demand trailing in its wake. And while rising domestic demand would have been expected to open up opportunities for expanding local agriculture by Chinese farmers, China's physical constraints – despite its geographic size, it has only 7 per cent of the world's arable land – and its rapid industrialisation and accompanying urbanisation over the last few decades have removed tens of thousands of hectares of fertile land from production. For China in particular, the fear that inflation and dwindling supplies could contribute to periodic waves of domestic unrest that had begun to gather force was underscored in a report issued by the state council on food security in 2005, the first year China became a major importer of food since the CPC took power. Following up on this, the National Development and Reform Commission produced a 20-year food security strategy whose preliminary findings were released in November 2008, setting out the parameters of food security for the country as being met first and foremost through the maintenance of 125 million hectares of arable land and 95 per cent self-sufficiency in grains (Kelley 2009: 94).

The African resource bounty

Against this backdrop, Africa has assumed a critical role in China's search for resource security. The African continent possesses a generous endowment in natural resources, namely hydrocarbons, minerals and timber, which remain mostly untapped due to decades of political instability, poor infrastructure and lack of investment. However, Chinese foray into this sector had to take into account the prevailing dominance of established interests, primarily from the US, France and Great Britain, all of which produced a pattern of investment that replicated colonial era divisions refracted through the politics of the cold war. This scenario sets the ground for growing competition for economic and political influence over the continent in the coming decades, which is particularly astounding if one considers that less than a decade ago the African continent was suffering from a sharp decline in interest from its traditional Western partners.

In regional terms Africa accounted for 9.5 per cent of global known oil deposits in 2010. Noteworthy is the fact that Africa boasts the fastest growth rate in oil reserves, having doubled in the past two decades. The largest reserves are located in Libya (46.4 billion barrels), Nigeria (37.2), Angola (13.5) and Algeria (12.2). In terms of production Africa ranks third with 12.2 per cent of the world total but the country ranking changes a bit with Nigeria as the main African oil producer (2.4 million bpd), followed by Angola (1.9 million bpd), Algeria (1.8 million bpd) and Libya (1.7 million bpd) (BP 2011).

Africa's endowment in non-fuel minerals further complements the attractiveness of this picture in which South Africa appears as a prize since it sits on one of the world's richest mineral beds. Among other minerals, South Africa is leading producer of platinum (80 per cent of total production and 90 per cent of world reserves) and manganese (holds over 75 per cent of the world's reserve base) and second world gold producer (overtaken by Australia in 2007). Moreover, South Africa is a major coal producer and has developed the world's leading technology in converting coal to synfuels, introducing new possibilities for the coal-rich Chinese state. Recognition of this has factored into the joint venture between two Chinese firms and the South African parastatal, Sasol. By way of contrast, despite decades of neglect and internecine conflict, the Democratic Republic of Congo's (DRC) mineral wealth is notoriously unexploited. Even so, DRC is the leading cobalt producer (36 per cent), possessing half of the world's known reserves, and also number one diamond producer (33 per cent of the total). With DRC, South Africa and Botswana jointly account for over half of global diamond mining output and 60 per cent of known deposits.[7] Among other African countries with significant reserves of minerals that have attracted Chinese interest are Gabon (manganese), Zambia (copper and iron ore), Zimbabwe (platinum) and Angola (diamonds, copper and iron ore).

Finally, African agriculture and forestry resources remain underdeveloped. According to the FAO, only 14 per cent of Africa's total 184 million hectares of available land is under cultivation, with 93 per cent of that dependent upon rainfall and fertiliser (Diouf 2008). African agriculture, which continues to serve as a mainstay of employment in most African countries, suffers from low productivity, chronic under-investment and difficulties in accessing potential foreign export markets. To be sure, the environmental constraints on agriculture in much of the continent are considerable, though viewed from a Chinese perspective these sorts of impediments are familiar ones. Private Chinese farmers have already set up farms in Uganda, South Africa and Zambia while larger agricultural firms are in negotiations with African governments to lease larger tracts of land for production. In terms of forestry, hundreds of thousands of square kilometres of virgin timber abound in parts of tropical Africa and have inspired China's small and medium sized companies to set up logging operations – both legal and illegal – across the continent.

Building on these broad-based economic complementarities between Africa as resource provider and China as resource consumer is the dramatic surge in trade. Between 1995 and 2000 commercial exchanges more than doubled from $4 billion to $10 billion; they quadrupled in the following five years to $42 billion in 2005, the figure surpassed $106 billion in 2008 and reached $160 billion in 2011. China currently accounts for 18 per cent of Africa's total trade, up from 8 per cent in 2008. In 2011 its share of African imports was 17 per cent (4.5 per cent in 2001) while absorbing 18 per cent of the continent's exports (up from 10 per cent in 2008) (Freemantle and Stevens 2012: 1–4).

New markets and diplomacy

Though resource security impulses are at the forefront of the contemporary push into Africa, with China's energy state-owned enterprises (SOE) taking the lead, the desire to take advantage of commercial opportunities by expanding trade into African markets has also played an important role. In part, the policy of using Chinese finance to support Chinese construction firms building infrastructure in Africa represents a concerted strategy of risk mitigation and, concurrently, provides incentives for domestic firms to go out and seek opportunities abroad. Indeed, survey data suggests that once established in the African market, Chinese firms 'anticipated that they will secure further contracts' (Davies and Corkin 2007: 246). The over-supply of infrastructure firms and labour within China itself provides an additional rationale for this expansion into new markets. The appeal for African governments of this approach, despite the concerns around the use of Chinese labour voiced in some circles, was that these were 'turnkey' operations that placed few demands on the African recipients and produced in short order a relatively inexpensive and functioning road, railroad, bridge or dam (Fletcher 2010: 7).

Another driver is the need by Chinese manufacturing firms to find new outlets for their products, with those operating at the low end of the consumer market especially (which were losing favour domestically and held little appeal in the more sophisticated Western markets) contributing to an overall surge in two-way trade (Broadman 2007). With manufacturing accounting for 32 per cent of China's GDP and 89 per cent of its merchandise exports by 2005, the importance of opening up new opportunities abroad was paramount (Biacuana et al 2009: 10). At a different level, a new wave of Chinese migrants have opened wholesale and retail shops across the continent, bringing low-cost goods to the African consumer and contributing to a boom in the purchase of items such as bicycles, radios and watches that were once out of reach of ordinary Africans.[8]

More traditional concerns around diplomacy featured as well in the contemporary Chinese movement into Africa. These included the longstanding competition with Taiwan for diplomatic recognition, with China able to retain or win recognition from a number of African states over the years (Rawnsley 2000). Beijing's drive to isolate the rebel province internationally meant that it actively sought to provide inducements for African governments to reconsider their links with Taipei. And finally, as pressure on China to play a more activist role on the global stage increased, the need to seek out partnerships with like-minded states became an imperative. Africa's position as a friendly environment for Beijing was underscored by its unwillingness to join in the Western sanctions campaign that followed in the wake of Tiananmen Square and its support for China in international forums as varied as the International Olympic Committee (where African votes helped secure Beijing's hosting of the 2008 Olympics) and the UN's Human Rights Commission. Sharing a common view on sovereignty and human rights – though one that was arguably in the process of changing with the establishment of the African Union and the emergence of the 'responsibility to protect' doctrine – enabled China to work in tandem on many issues with the largest regional voting bloc in the UN (Alden 2007: 16).

The Chinese in Africa from state-owned enterprises to shopkeepers

Capturing the diversity of China's engagement in Africa is necessary to achieve any understanding of the complex and sometimes contrary reactions that its presence inspires across Africa. Ranging from global parastatals like China National Offshore Oil Corporation (CNOOC) to thousands of retail shops, the Chinese have made inroads in the economic life of ordinary Africans in an extraordinarily short period of time. Moreover, the rapidity with which these Chinese actors adapt to changing circumstances in Africa – in some part a product of the fast pace of change in China itself – continually challenges assumptions about their standing in Africa.

At the sharp end of China's engagement in Africa are a host of SOEs which have sought to gain access to resources and markets formerly dominated by Western and South African firms. Using a package of high-profile diplomatic and substantive financial incentives, these SOEs have been able to secure leases for oil in Angola, Sudan and Nigeria as well as deals gaining access to strategic minerals in countries such as Gabon, DRC and Zimbabwe.

The proximity of top management of these SOEs to leading party officials, according to one study, 'affords certain strategic SOEs vital political connections and a measure of input into foreign policy decisions pertaining to their particular business interests' (Jakobson and Know 2010: 26). For developmentally-minded African leaders, the attractiveness of Chinese support for infrastructure development, an area neglected by traditional Western donors in recent decades, is rooted in the visible and immediate impact that provisions for transportation and communication have on enhancing the economic potential in their respective countries as well as improving livelihoods within affected communities. These 'resources for infrastructure' deals, often involving billions of dollars-worth of low concessional loans by China Exim Bank, have been carried out for the most part by Chinese construction firms whose use of contracted labourers and even basic supplies has been criticised in some African circles.

Moreover, the overall competitiveness of Chinese firms has meant that, once exposed to the African environment, they have been able to capture a growing portion of the open-tenders-for-infrastructure projects. According to one study, Chinese construction firms have succeeded in recent years in winning 30 per cent of the combined value of infrastructure contracts tendered by the African Development Bank and World Bank (Foster et al 2007: 5–6). This trend is evident in the conduct of Chinese infrastructure and engineering firms operating in Africa as early as 1988 where in Liberia, for example, the China State Construction Engineering Corporation was able to stay on and win contracts from the Liberian government to renovate the local hospital (Brautigam 1998: 214). Contemporary examples of Chinese construction firms entering African markets via a Chinese-financed project and winning public tenders abound. And, as their personal contracts are completed, an undetermined number of Chinese labourers brought in to work on these construction projects have stayed on in Africa to seek out employment opportunities or open up small businesses.

Indeed, while Chinese SOEs captivate the attention of the international media, there is an equivalent drive by small and medium enterprises into the continent which is as prevalent and arguably making as much of an impact as the aspiring multinationals. Many of the medium-sized companies are drawn from the ranks of the rehabilitated SOE sector, which has been undergoing a painful restructuring process that has cut it back from 300,000 to 150,000 firms over the last decade (CSIS/IIE 2006: 23–24).[9] In some cases these businesses were motivated by a desire on the part of a relatively large Chinese company to establish foreign subsidiaries so as to guarantee access to Western markets should protectionism take root (Hong and Sun 2006: 624). For many smaller businesses, the motivation, as noted above, is to make use of China's advantage relative to African companies where they possess relatively advanced technologies and cost-effective production that gives them a competitive edge over locals and foreign firms (Hong and Sun 2006: 625). This market-seeking impulse is borne out in surveys conducted of 80 Chinese small and medium enterprises (SME) working in Africa which ranked gaining access to the continent's markets as their top rationale (Jing 2009: 570–585).

At the same time, the poor conduct of some Chinese firms operating in Africa has threatened to tarnish the overall reputation of China. For instance, the willingness to ignore basic health and safety regulations, local labour laws and even environmental standards within the industry by a number of Chinese mining companies based in Katanga province, DRC, has brought down a rain of criticism (*Bloomberg* 2008). The fact that the collapse in commodity prices in late 2008 caused many of these companies to pull out of DRC only highlights their opportunistic and exploitative character. And in Zambia, for many Chinese an exemplary African partner, the poor practices of a leading Chinese mining firm resulted in a spate of accidental deaths in 2006 and, in 2010, the shooting of 11 African labourers by Chinese managers during a labour dispute.

Finally, the growing trend of Chinese migration in parts of Africa has not passed unnoticed in communities unaccustomed to hosting foreigners from beyond the continent. Much of the Chinese immigration has been undocumented, leading to wild speculation as to the numbers of Chinese settling in the continent, a situation further compounded by the African tendency to identify all non-Indian Asians as Chinese. Within the continent's leading migration destination, South Africa, the Chinese community has surged from 80,000 in the 1980s to an estimated 350,000 in 2006, though overall migration to Africa is declared by Beijing to be only 750,000 (the evacuation of over 35,000 Chinese from Libya in early 2011, however, in itself suggests the official figures are very understated) (Park 2009: 3). Concurrently, the evident lack of financial means and weak skill base of many of the migrants has raised concerns amongst educated Africans and small business owners alike. The proliferation of Chinese retail shops in urban and rural communities, bringing access to low-cost consumer goods in African markets for the first time, is nonetheless driving Africans out of the retail trade and, in so doing, spurring resentment in these circles.

In short, during the last decade and a half, the Chinese presence in Africa has been marked by diversity in composition and depth, defying the easy stereotypes that have accompanied many portrayals in the Western and even African media. This spectrum of Chinese actors has been further matched by changing approaches to Africa at the highest levels by authorities in Beijing and, more prosaically, by individual migration strategies. Africa's resources may be the instigator of Chinese interests but it is clear that China's ties with the continent are increasingly set to be anchored by an expanding cast of characters and changing relationships.

The diplomatic cornerstone of the relationship

A special dimension of China's engagement with the African continent has been the founding of a regionally tailored multilateral platform, the Forum for China–Africa Cooperation (FOCAC), in 2000. This regularised structure provides a public setting for celebrating the achievements of the relationship, an opportunity to formulate a raft of economic targets aimed at fostering mutual development interests and recalibrating policies to match these, as well as a stage to endorse common perspectives on global issues. At the same time, while multilateralism characterises this public diplomacy of the China–Africa relationship, most of the substance of economic ties (notably aid and investment agreements) continues to be rooted in bilateral relations between China and individual African states.

What is striking about the FOCAC IV ministerial meeting held in November 2009 is the degree to which, building upon the first three FOCAC meetings, this process reflects a growing and deliberately constructed convergence between African development needs and Chinese economic interests. For instance, in agriculture – long recognised to be a sector where Africa's potential comparative advantages have remained under-invested and under-utilised (and one in which the Chinese have provided technical assistance since the 1960s) – the Chinese propose to introduce new techniques, seed varieties and training programmes which are derived from their own experience of raising productivity amongst their farmers.[10] To facilitate this process, the Chinese government is rolling out an additional ten agricultural training centres across the continent in countries like Mozambique, Zimbabwe and Senegal. Coupled to this are additional means aimed at providing financial support for commercial enterprises. Raising Africa's agricultural productivity will not only dramatically enhance the livelihoods of rural communities in Africa through improvements in income generation and employment, but can also address a growing problem of food security in China itself.

Another example is the targeting of Africa's small and medium enterprises for development and growth through a special $1 billion special fund. Moreover, signalling that they understand that a focus on the supply side is not enough to make real development gains, Beijing has agreed to scrap tariffs on 95 per cent of all products from Africa's less developed countries. This decision to open up China's market to African commerce has the potential, when linked with the support for African business, to set off a virtuous chain of development. The redirecting of African capabilities towards accessing the Chinese market could lay the foundation for a more balanced, long-term trading relationship than has been the case so far. At the same time, it bears mentioning that it could end up like the US African Growth and Opportunity Act (AGOA), which gave preferential access to the American market in sectors like clothing that contributed to a surge not so much in African but rather Asian-based investment. Africans will have to be nimble investors to make the most out of what seem to be genuinely liberal terms on offer. Indeed, they may even find that they are competing with the growing Chinese communities within their midst whose proven entrepreneurial acumen and understanding of the Chinese domestic market has fuelled China's own economic transformation.

Moreover, the diversity of Chinese actors in Africa – contrary to the presumptions of the notion of 'China–Africa' as comprising two unitary entities – poses a dilemma in structuring and managing the relationship. Once shaped and led at the top by Beijing's political elites in conjunction with their African counterparts, the steady diffusion of economic power to semi-autonomous SOEs, provincial authorities and a sometimes rapacious profit-seeking private sector has introduced diversity of interests and practice that are as often at odds with Chinese foreign policy aims as they are aligned with them. Estimates suggest that there are over 20,000 SMEs operating in Africa today (Jing 2009: 570–85).

This situation also highlights one of the most notable gaps in the FOCAC process, that is the role of actors formally outside of the state. While much of the media attention was focused on what happened within the halls of the FOCAC ministerial and the press conferences, the FOCAC business forum met on the fringes of the event. Missing, however, was the once mooted inclusion of a parallel Chinese–African civil society process. In the Western context, the role of guardian of the underlying values which inform national foreign policies is partially played by a vibrant and active civil society operating both in the West and in Africa. Unabashedly critical of the state and private capital – and undoubtedly the bane of authoritarian and, at times, democratic governments alike – these sometimes self-appointed 'voices of the people' nonetheless serve a tremendously important function in reasserting the moral purpose of foreign policy actions. In Africa, China has seemingly exported many features of its domestic setting (such as opaque business and financial practices) and this includes a weak civil society whose boundaries of action are circumscribed to varying degrees by the state. Whether the current situation, which places the burden of responsibility solely on the CPC leadership and bureaucracy to anticipate, manage and ameliorate the conduct of a plethora of Chinese actors in Africa, is sufficient remains to be seen.

Conclusion

China's emergence as a leading trade and investment partner with Africa has revived the flagging fortunes of Africa's resource-based economies, providing new investment and new markets that have contributed to the global commodity boom. In political terms, the African example suggests that China can provide a welcome alternative to the longstanding paternalistic relationship with Western governments. However, the belated recognition that African political instability has a negative impact on Chinese economic interests is raising concerns in Beijing as it seeks to find a way to balance its new role in Africa.

At the same time, change and adaptability remain the hall-marks of China–Africa relations and, to the credit of the Chinese government whose willingness to revisit and revise specific initiatives in light of experience on the ground, give the relationship – and FOCAC in particular – a dynamism lacking in many other trans-regional initiatives. China's willingness to maintain its focus on building a long term economic relationship with the African continent, despite the adverse global economic climate, makes such negotiations all the more important for Africa. But coming to terms with the diversity of Chinese actors and their narrower, and often self-serving, interests are a challenge to ensuring that this carefully constructed relationship with this developing region stays on course.

Notes

1. For further details on this see Alden (2007).
2. For a detailed account on energy security emergence as China's foreign policy major driver see Zweig and Jianhai (2005).
3. China occupies the fifth position as producer after the Russian Federation (12.9 per cent), Saudi Arabia (12 per cent), US (8.7 per cent) and Iran (5.2 per cent). Data according to BP, 'Statistical Review of world energy' 2011, http://www.bp.com/sectionbodycopy.do?categoryId=7500&contentId=7068481, accessed 30 March 2012.
4. US refinery capacity share is 19.2 per cent of total. Ibid
5. According to BP, in 2010 China produced 4.1 million bpd and consumed 9.1 million bpd. Ibid.
6. http://www.china.org.cn/english/environment/236955.htm, accessed 27 February 2012.
7. Figures according to data of the Chinese Ministry of Commerce (2008)

and WTO data in: http://www.wto.org/english/res_e/statis_e/its2006_e/appendix_e/a14.xls, accessed 27 February 2012.

8. See, for instance, Dittigen (2010), Park (2009), Dobler (2008).
9. At a cost of 25 million unemployed, this sector having formerly employed 80 per cent of all of Chinese workers.
10. For an overview of Chinese technical assistance in the agricultural sector in Africa see Brautigam (1998).

References

Alden, C. (2007) *China in Africa*, London, Zed Books

Biacuana, G., Disenyana, T., Draper, P. and Khumalo, N. (2009) 'China's manufacturing exports and Africa's deindustrialisation', Johannesburg, SAIIA

Bloomberg (2008) 'China lets child workers die digging in Congo mines for copper', 22 June, http://www.bloomberg.com/apps/news?pid=newsarchive&sid=aW8xVLQ4Xhr8, accessed 27 February 2012

BP (2011) 'Statistical Review of World Energy' http://www.bp.com/sectionbodycopy.do?categoryId=7500&contentId=7068481 ,accessed 30 March 2012

Brautigam, D. (1998) *Chinese Aid and African Development: Exporting Green Revolution*, Basingstoke, Palgrave Macmillan

Brett, D. and Ericsson, M. (2006) 'Chinese expansion to create new global mining companies', *Commodities Now*, October http://www.rmg.se/RMG2005/pages/attachments/COMMODITIES_NOW_2006_Oct,_Chinese_Expansion_to_Create_New_Global_Mining_Companies.pdf, accessed 27 February 2012

Broadman, H. (2007) *Africa's Silk Road*, Washington DC, World Bank

Chinese Ministry of Commerce (2008) http://english.mofcom.gov.cn/article/statistic/ie/200802/20080205371690.html, accessed 27 February 2012

CSIS/IIE (2006) *China: the Balance Sheet*, Washington DC, Center for Strategic and International Studies/Institute for International Economics

Davies, M. and Corkin, L. (2007) 'China's entry into Africa's construction sector: the case of Angola', in le Pere, G. (ed.) *China in Africa: Mercantilist Predator or Partner in Development?*, Midrand, SAIIA/IGD

Diouf, J. (2008), 'Africa: director general addresses the FAO regional conference for Africa', 19 June, http://allafrica.com/stories/200806191059.html, accessed 5 March 2012

Dittigen, R. (2010) 'From isolation to integration? A study of Chinese retailers in Dakar', *SAIIA Occasional Paper*, 57

Dobler, G. (2008) 'Solidarity, xenophobia and the regulation of Chinese businesses in Namibia', in Alden, C., Large, D. and Soares de Oliveira, R. (eds), *China Returns to Africa: an Emerging Power and a Continent Embrace*, London, Hurst

Fletcher, H. (2010) 'Development aid for infrastructure investment in Africa: Malian relations with China, the European Commission and the World Bank', *SAIIA Occasional Paper*, 58

Foster, V., Butterfield, W., Chen, C. and Pushka, N. (2007) *Building Bridges: China's Growing Role as Infrastructure Financier in Africa*, World Bank and PPIAF Washington DC

Freemantle, S. and Stevens, J. (2012), 'China–Africa: taking stock after a decade of advance', Africa Insight and Strategy, Standard Bank, 19 March, http://bit.ly/HTYdln, accessed 4 April 2012

Goldstein, A., Pinaud, P., Reisen, H. and Chen, X. (2006) *The Rise of China and India: What's in it for Africa?*, Paris, OECD

Hong, E. and Sun, L. (2006) 'Dynamics of Iinternationalisation and outward investment: Chinese corporations' strategies', *The China Quarterly*, 187

Hsiao, R. (2008) 'Energy security the centrepiece of China's foreign policy', *China Brief*, 8, http://www.jamestown.org/single/?no_cache=1&tx_ttnews%5Btt_news%5D=5095, accessed 11 April 2012

Jakobson, L. and Know, D. (2010) 'New foreign policy actors in China', *Policy Paper 26*, SIPRI

Jing, G. (2009) 'China's private enterprises in Africa and the implications for African development', *European Journal of Development Research*, 21(4)

Kelley, J. (2009) 'International Institute for Environment and Development, in testimony before the European Union Committee, House of Lords,' 7th Report of Session 2009–10, Volume II: evidence, 30 April

OPEC (2011), 'Oil supply and demand outlook to 2035', http://www.opec.org/opec_web/static_files_project/media/downloads/publications/WOOSectionOne2011.pdf, accessed 15 May 2012

Park, Y. (2009) 'Chinese migration in Africa', *SAIIA Occasional Paper*, 24

Rawnsley, G. (2000) *Taiwan's Informal Diplomacy and Propaganda*, Basingstoke, Macmillan

Soares de Oliveira, R. (2008) 'Making sense of Chinese oil investment in Africa' in Alden, C., Large, D. and Soares de Oliveira, R. (eds), *China Returns to Africa: an Emerging Power and a Continent Embrace*, London, Hurst

Zweig, D. and Jianhai, B. (2005) 'China's global hunt for energy', *Foreign Affairs* 84(5)

2

China is Angola's new best friend – for now

Assis Malaquias

Introduction

The dominant narrative on Sino-Angolan relations suggests that both sides come out as winners. China benefits because Angola is a willing supplier of oil to help fuel China's impressive economic growth. Angola wins because China provides critical assistance in Angola's post-war reconstruction process. Thus, the narrative posits, there exists a base for an enduring strategic partnership between the two countries. This chapter suggests that this is accurate but only if the analysis is confined to government-to-government relations. A broader and more careful analysis of this complex relationship would have to include how the relations between China and Angola affect the Angolan state and society. Such an analysis yields a richer, if more troubling, picture.

Undoubtedly, the Angolan government stands to gain significant and immediate benefits from this relationship. The end of the civil war a decade ago significantly raised Angolans' expectations about their government's commitment to taking specific steps to improve their lives. For more than thirty years, the government routinely used the civil war as a justification for its poor performance. The absence of war both nullified the powerful no-resources-for-development argument and increased the political risks associated with the government's many governance weaknesses, especially regarding resource management. This would have potentially explosive consequences given high levels of poverty and equally high expectations for post-conflict development.

From this perspective, the partnership with China represents an optimal immediate mechanism enabling the Angolan government to deliver the goods and thus assure continued legitimacy.

However, from a broader society level, an assessment of the Sino-Angolan relationship must incorporate each country's development goals and the models they have adopted to achieve these goals. Some observers of Sino-African relations have pointed out that the Chinese model's appeal in Africa rests on its ability to provide both rapid economic growth and political stability (Kurlantzick 2006, Konings 2007, Obiorah 2008). But this model is problematic in places where society demands both economic prosperity and political freedoms. In the case of Angola, at independence most citizens took it for granted that the country's immense natural resource endowment – including vast oil reserves, extensive diamond deposits and rich agricultural land – would serve as the basis for post-colonial economic prosperity. This was postponed by three decades of civil war that started in the run-up to independence. Problematically for Angola, the post-colonial period was marked by civil war as well as single-party politics and centralised economic planning.

The transitions from war to peace, from single-party to multi-party politics, and from centralised to free market economics were supposed to have taken place in the late 1980s and early 1990s when Angola changed its post-colonial trajectory due to the collapse of its main benefactor and ideological guide – the former Soviet Union – and the end of the cold war. Without military support from the Soviet Union, the governing Movimento Popular de Libertação de Angola (MPLA) could not aspire to emerge triumphant in the civil war because its opponent, the União Nacional para Independência Total de Angola (UNITA), was supported by the only remaining superpower, the United States. Thus, MPLA opted for a negotiated end of the conflict and to take its chances at the ballot box instead of risking outright military defeat. The end of the civil war necessitated opening the political space to opposition parties, including a militarily powerful UNITA. Likewise, greater political freedoms had to go hand in hand with economic liberalisation. The political and economic transitions, albeit problematic in the sense that they did not fully succeed in breaking MPLA's stranglehold on the key levers of power, gained some momentum during the 1990s. But the resumption of the civil war in 1992, after a failed internationally backed peace process, postponed the key transition from war to peace by a decade. The death of UNITA rebel leader Jonas Savimbi in 2002 created the conditions for the war to end and gave Angola another chance to attempt the three transitions simultaneously. Importantly, the end of the war has emboldened both opposition parties and civil society organisations to demand greater transparency in government as a condition for building a more just and democratic society.

Having taken the important initial first steps toward democracy and free markets, it is unlikely that Angolan society will embrace the Chinese model of governance, based as it is on strict one-party control, even if that system also produces fast economic growth. This suggests that China is not Angola's ideal long-term partner because they are on different development trajectories. From this perspective, several key international players – including South Africa, Brazil and the United States – are more suitable long-term strategic partners because their political and economic systems are better aligned with those Angola aspires to build. In other words, the Angolan government will pursue short-term objectives with China. However, in the long run, Angola–China relations will be viewed – much like Angola's past relations with Cuba and the former Soviet Union – as a critical instrument to enable Angola to face pressing internal challenges. Angola's intent is not necessarily to establish a privileged long-term strategic relationship with China.

The current Angola–China strategic partnership will be tested for two reasons. First, despite the magnitude of the post-conflict rebuilding efforts being financed by Chinese capital, the expectations and aspirations of Angolans are too great to be adequately satisfied in the near future. Second, as recent events in Angola attest (Pawson 2011), its citizens are becoming increasingly dissatisfied with a regime that many consider to be corrupt and dictatorial. To survive growing domestic pressures to satisfy both economic and political aspirations of the citizenry, the governing MPLA is likely to use pragmatism again as its main compass, as it moves away from heavy reliance on the Asian giant towards closer relations with the United States and other mature democracies (Malaquias 2011).

Angola's difficult post-colonial first steps

The choices made by the Angolan state since independence reflect the orientation of its leading political force, the governing MPLA. Although this movement participated in the anti-colonial struggle with two other nationalist groups – Frente Nacional de Libertação de Angola (FNLA) and UNITA – MPLA was able to manoeuvre itself into a commanding political and military position from which it was able to receive power from the departing colonial authorities. MPLA had several important advantages. First, it had a clear and well-articulated programme of national liberation and operated as an inclusive organisation that, while heavily influenced by communist ideology, congregated all socio-economic, ethnic, and racial segments of colonial society. Second, its ideological leanings and cosmopolitan composition made it the favourite interlocutor for the equally leftist Armed Forces Movement in Portugal that overthrew the fascist regime in the colonial metropolis in 1974, setting in motion the decolonisation process. Third, MPLA had key international friends – including the former Soviet Union and Cuba – who were willing to provide resources such as troops, material, and money in sufficient quantities to ensure that MPLA prevailed over its domestic and foreign adversaries. Thus, despite the chaotic process, MPLA was the only liberation movement in power when the decolonisation dust settled.

Once in government, however, MPLA quickly realised that it faced a series of daunting challenges to remain in power and build the post-colonial state it had outlined in its liberation programme. First, the violence that surrounded much of the decolonisation process forced the vast majority of the settlers to leave the country, mainly back to Portugal. The removal of an entire segment of the population with a predominantly unfavourable disposition toward the new rulers might not have been an entirely undesirable outcome but for the fact that, due to severely discriminatory policies, the colonial administration had reserved nearly all education opportunities for the settler population. Thus, in leaving, the settler population was taking with them all the essential skills necessary for the functioning of a modern society. Consequently, most economic activity outside the oil sector rapidly ground to a halt.

Second, the other two liberation movements did not leave the stage quietly. Both FNLA and UNITA attempted to prevent MPLA from gaining control of the capital city to declare independence in November 1975. MPLA fought back ferociously and was able to inflict a devastating military blow from which FNLA never fully recovered. By 1978, FNLA was a spent political and military force with many of its members having fled into exile in neighbouring Zaire (present-day Democratic Republic of Congo) while others found refuge farther afield, all the way to Europe and even the United States. The third major nationalist movement, UNITA, proved to be a more resilient foe. It was able to survive intense military punishment at the hands of MPLA and retreated to sparsely populated regions of south-eastern Angola from where it mounted a formidable military opposition to the new regime with considerable external support, including from South Africa and the United States. By the mid-1980s, UNITA had succeeded in putting MPLA on the defensive, having pushed most government forces into the relative security of major urban areas. This pressure on the ground, coupled with the end of the cold war and the former Soviet Union's disengagement from conflicts like Angola, encouraged the MPLA government to accept the internationally backed peace talks with UNITA that culminated in the Bicesse Peace Accords of 1991. Peace, alas, lasted for only a year. As noted above, a new and even more devastating phase of the civil war would last for another decade.

Third, the main regional powers, particularly apartheid South Africa, continued to overtly destabilise the new state because the revolutionary regime in Luanda saw itself as part of a larger liberation movement in southern Africa. For much of the late 1970s and through the 1980s, South Africa carried out regular military operations deep inside Angola for two main reasons: to weaken the South West Africa People's Organisation (SWAPO), the Namibian liberation movement, and disrupt the Namibian rebels' military operations by attacking their bases in Angola and, simultaneously, to strengthen UNITA by providing the Angolan rebels with direct assistance to expand their areas of operation and protect them whenever they were endangered by advancing Angolan government troops.

Fourth, within the prevailing cold war context, Angola's condition as a Soviet client and Cuban ally meant that it did not have many allies in the West. Certainly, it could not count the United States as a friend. Given MPLA's communist origins, its initial attempts to establish contacts with the US received a frosty reception. Instead, the US opened channels to MPLA's opponents: FNLA in the 1960s and UNITA in the 1970s. By the time MPLA replaced the departing colonial administration in 1975, US assistance to FNLA and UNITA ensured that MPLA's grip on power in Angola was tenuous, at best. Thus, at independence, the MPLA government faced challenging problems for which it was not always able to provide the best solution.

Options at independence

Although difficult circumstances conspired against the new Angolan state from its birth, the choices made by the new government compounded an already difficult situation. Politically, the winner-take-all approach ensured that those Angolans who did not belong to MPLA had few incentives to cooperate in building a new state. Many, especially those who belonged to the liberation movements defeated in the civil war – UNITA members in particular – successfully found in MPLA's rigid single-party exclusionary politics a powerful justification for using military means in their attempt to overthrow the government.

Economically, the new government introduced measures that forced the country deeper into the abyss. Already reeling from the effects of the settler exodus, the economy was dealt another massive blow when the government instituted policies aimed at creating a centrally planned economy. The nationalisation of nearly all economic activity severely devastated the economy, forcing it into depths from which it would not recover for three decades. Further exacerbating the situation, the new regime's ideological preference for the socio-economic classes most oppressed under colonialism – peasants and the urban working classes – meant that the few Angolans with an education – the new 'petite bourgeoisie' – were now both despised and marginalised. Many joined the settlers' exodus. The few who stayed behind suffered further reprisals when, in the aftermath of an attempted coup d'état in 1977, the regime conveniently used them as scapegoats. In many ways, the state avoided collapse only due to the influx of thousands of civilian advisers from the Soviet Union and satellite states as well as an even larger contingent of Cuban troops.

Although the state was able to survive, the pro-peasant and working class bias had several long-lasting unintended consequences. One consequence was felt in the state's poor performance in creating the conditions for the training of qualified individuals to replace the settlers who left at independence as well as the Soviet, Cuban, and other allies who sooner or later would similarly depart. The post-independence Angolan government opted to expand education opportunities both for the school-age children of previously underprivileged classes as well as for the vast majority of citizens who were illiterate. Thus, the government made education for the first four years compulsory. In addition, it started an ambitious national adult literacy campaign. But the government did not have the resources – either human or financial – to match its goals. Since the colonial regime provided few educational opportunities for indigenous Angolans, there were few qualified teachers and school administrators available to support the government's ambitious education policies. The government's attempt to mitigate this shortage with Cuban teachers proved problematic from the beginning, mainly due to language differences (Spanish-speaking Cuban teachers and Portuguese-speaking students), lack of basic infrastructure (not nearly enough schools to accommodate the large number of new students), and insecurity (beginning in the late 1970s, many of Angola's rural areas were ravaged by UNITA's growing insurgency). The Cuban teachers eventually left in the mid-1980s, leaving behind a barely functioning educational system that was unable to provide students with the skills needed to replace the Portuguese settlers. Likewise, their departing military compatriots left the Angolan government contemplating difficult choices as it looked for ways to remain in power. How did MPLA manage to survive?

MPLA's survival strategies

Confronted with complex and multilayered crises, MPLA survived by pursuing several simultaneous strategies. Internally, the leadership used public funds from abundant oil revenues to lavishly pay those who constituted the regime's main pillars, i.e.

the governing party and government officials as well as security sector officers who, in turn, were expected to look after their own trusted circle of supporters. Thus, the MPLA leadership ensured that hundreds of thousands of its supporters had a personal stake, not just an ideological inclination, in ensuring regime survival. The corruption that now defines governance in Angola – where the unaccountable use of public funds for personal enrichment has become the norm – is a direct consequence of this survival strategy.

For MPLA in the late 1970s and through the 80s, internal survival was intimately connected to international and regional dynamics. At the international level, the MPLA regime carefully developed strong relationships with what were formerly known as the Eastern Bloc countries, especially with the former Soviet Union and Cuba, to ensure survival. At the regional level, the new regime spared no diplomatic efforts or resources – neither financial nor military – to change the regional security environment to its advantage. Specifically, it provided the liberation movements in Namibia and South Africa with the means they needed to force the apartheid regime to relinquish control over Namibia and, later, to relinquish power altogether. With an independent Namibia, the main staging point for South Africa's regular incursion into Angola in support of UNITA was no longer available. Later, with the collapse of the apartheid regime in 1994, UNITA would be left without its most important regional backer. In 1997, Angola played a key role in removing president Mobutu of Zaire from power and installing a friendly regime in Kinshasa. Although the MPLA was able to cling to power, its grip appeared increasingly tenuous as UNITA rebels grew in military strength during the 1980s as a result of considerable assistance from South Africa and the United States. Thus, with the end of the cold war and Soviet–Cuban disengagement, the MPLA government had little choice but to accept an internationally backed plan to end the civil war through negotiations with UNITA. The resulting Bicesse Peace Accords paved the way to Angola's first multi-party elections in 1992. But the elections did not end the civil war because the political stakes for which MPLA and UNITA had been fighting each other since independence had not been lowered during the Bicesse process. Shortsightedly, the negotiations focused almost exclusively on ending the protracted civil war. In many ways, this constituted a repeat of the misjudgements that had led to the civil war in the first place. By focusing on mechanisms each believed could be used to strengthen their respective positions to ultimately prevail over the other – the transitional government in 1975 and elections in 1992 – MPLA and UNITA failed to devise a system whereby power and wealth were distributed equitably enough to ensure sustainable peace. In other words, the negotiators at Bicesse lacked the will or the creativity to develop the foundations of a political system where both winners and losers had a high stake, i.e. a system that could compel MPLA and UNITA to work together. Predictably, the Bicesse Peace Accords failed catastrophically. Although elections were held, the results did not bring peace. Rather, expectedly, the losers – Jonas Savimbi and his UNITA – rejected the results which they claimed to have been rigged. No conclusive evidence of vote rigging was ever presented. But this was beside the point. Savimbi and UNITA could not have accepted election results that confirmed their defeat at the ballot box – something MPLA had not been able to accomplish on the battlefield. For a rebel army masquerading as a political party, this was simply unacceptable. Thus, for the following decade, the rebels mounted a furious, if ultimately unsuccessful, military campaign against the government. Although the government survived, few of the country's infrastructures did. Using millions of dollars in revenues derived from diamonds illegally mined in areas under their control, the rebels were able to acquire an impressive arsenal – including tanks and heavy artillery – which they used indiscriminately on military and civilian targets around the country.

When the civil war finally ended in 2002 after nearly three decades, the country was completely exhausted and severely devastated. Having survived the military challenge posed by the rebels, there was no certainty that MPLA would be equally successful in surviving the political challenges inherent in the colossal task of rebuilding a destroyed country. They needed to build the foundations for a future that could fulfil the very high expectations of citizens who were both tired of war and eager to have a piece of the good life previously enjoyed mainly by the ruling elites. Failure to quickly expand social services to the population – especially access to housing, healthcare, clean water, and electricity – could trigger the kind of potentially explosive social instability that a highly militarised society emerging from a long civil war could ill afford.

Since, as noted above, MPLA's survival strategies involved the distribution of massive amounts of public funds to keep party and government officials as well as security sector officers happy at the centre of a vast patron-client network, very little was saved for the post-conflict reconstruction effort. Additionally, as survival was the overriding concern, little attention was focused on education and training. Thus, at the end of the war, the regime faced the stark reality that it lacked both the financial and the human resources to undertake the rebuilding process. Desperately, MPLA looked abroad for help.

No assistance from the West

With the end of the civil war, the Angolan government expected international sympathies to be translated into tangible offers of assistance, as it embarked on the colossal task of rebuilding the country. The government expected that Western countries, in particular, would rush in with assistance because they were perceived as being partly responsible for the destruction inflicted upon Angola, owing to their support for UNITA rebels during much of the conflict. The MPLA government vigorously lobbied for a donors' conference immediately after the war. Much to its disappointment, however, such a conference never took place. Western countries viewed the civil war as an internal Angolan matter and, therefore, dismissed suggestions of culpability or responsibility. Moreover, many Western governments found it difficult to justify spending taxpayers' funds to rebuild a resource-rich country that had developed a reputation as one of the most corrupt in the world. For the West, especially the United States, Angola's problem did not reside in the lack of funds but in their lack of a transparent government.

By withholding support for the donors' conference, the United States signalled displeasure with the Angolan government's lack of transparency in the management of public finances, especially of funds accrued from the sale of oil and diamonds. During the civil war, billions of dollars in oil revenues had bypassed the

National Bank of Angola[1] and were managed directly from the Futungo de Belas presidential palace. Human Rights Watch estimates that over a five-year period from 1997 to 2002, an estimated $4.2 billion in oil revenues 'disappeared from government coffers, roughly equal to all foreign and domestic social and humanitarian spending in Angola over that same period' (Human Rights Watch 2010). While consistently disapproving of corruption in Angola, the United States also encouraged the Angolan government to take concrete steps to improve governance. Tackling both ills – corruption and poor governance – would require sustained efforts by the Angolan government over a long time. But, with the end of the war and with the population expecting to see immediate action on development plans which the governing MPLA claimed not to have implemented due to the conflict, the Angolan government was not willing to bear the political cost of responding to Western demands. In other words, anti-corruption and good-governance measures could wait a little longer but ambitious reconstruction and development projects could not. Thus, the Angolan government sought international backers who demanded no more than access to natural resources in exchange for financial generosity. China was especially eager to finance Angola's reconstruction efforts and development plans.

China in Angola

Angola and China have formally agreed to establish a 'strategic partnership' (Xinhua 2010). This is further evidence of the importance both countries place on a relationship that has grown steadily since China granted diplomatic recognition to Angola in 1983 and has accelerated since the end of Angola's civil war. Angola is one of Africa's top oil producers, China's largest oil supplier on the continent, and China's largest trading partner in Africa.

Liberation struggle

China's relationship with Angola has a long history that can be traced back to the early stages of the liberation struggle against Portugal in the early 1960s. This involvement has consistently reflected both long-term strategic calculations and short-term pragmatism by the Chinese government. A long-term view resulted in China's careful and sustained engagement over the decades. These calculations were based on China's assessment of Angola's potential at various levels, especially as a supplier of raw materials, its geostrategic position in both central and southern Africa, and the likelihood of Angola playing a leadership role in either or both regions.

Pragmatic calculations enabled China to make and shift alliances with the three nationalist movements, depending on which appeared strongest at the time. China supported the MPLA in the early 1960s when this movement took the leading role in initiating the anti-colonial struggle. With the creation of the Revolutionary Government of Angola in Exile (GRAE)[2] by Holden Roberto in 1962, China shifted support towards this Angolan 'government'. In the mid-1960s Chinese assistance in the nationalist cause in Angola shifted again, this time towards Jonas Savimbi's embryonic movement, UNITA.[3] China's support of UNITA was not surprising. As a nationalist group, UNITA claimed to represent a significant segment of the population and was likely to have a prominent role in an independent state. In the 1970s, however, China hedged its bets by resuming its provision of assistance to Holden Roberto's FNLA. This time, China calculated that the militarily stronger movement,[4] the FNLA, was sure to play a key role both in the run-up to independence and in post-colonial Angola. In hindsight, China's early engagement in Angola was misguided because it was based on optimistic analysis of the transition to independence. It did not take into account the possibility of civil war and the triumph of military power, which was determined mainly by external intervention, in that transition. Consequently, in the end neither UNITA nor the FNLA was capable of achieving power by political or military means. Instead, power went to the nationalist movement that was supported by one of China's main nemeses. This partly explains China's long hiatus – 1975 to 2004 – from Angola.

China's big return

China returned to Angola in a major way in 2004. Two important sets of factors brought the two countries into this mutually beneficial relationship. As noted, at the end of the civil war in 2002, Angola was in desperate need of external support to initiate a massive post-conflict reconstruction programme. Concurrently, the then Chinese President Jiang Zemin (2002) announced his country's 'going out' strategy, intended to position China as a key player in the current phase of globalisation by extending and consolidating commercial links throughout the world.

At the end of the civil war, China provided Angola with vital financial and economic lifelines. Having saved very little during the post-independence period as a result of both war expenditures and rampant corruption, and having failed to convince Western countries that it was deserving of their financial assistance for post-conflict reconstruction, the Angolan government was faced with the frightening prospect of having to inaugurate a new era of peace and development without adequate financial resources. Thus, China's significant oil-backed line of credit to Angola could not have come at a better time for the MPLA government. But China's lifeline went far beyond the financial domain. Even with its immediate financial problems now resolved, Angola lacked the basic conditions, especially in terms of trained labour, to kick-start the reconstruction process. This is where China arguably played the most important role regarding Angola's post-conflict (re)building.

The Chinese companies chosen to execute the contracts financed by Chinese capital provided all the necessary inputs for the completion of said contracts, including labour and services. This is the main factor explaining the fast completion rate of the Chinese-financed projects. Other factors, including the Chinese companies' propensity to employ their labour in rotating teams, also played a significant role. It is not uncommon for Chinese companies to work on projects around the clock with teams of workers rotating every eight hours or so. Using this approach, Chinese companies quickly repaired destroyed transportation infrastructure including roads, railroads, ports, and airports. But they are also undertaking new projects around the country in most economic sectors. Housing, one of the hitherto most neglected sectors, has received special attention: extensive new urban developments have been rising outside Luanda and more are also being built elsewhere around the country. In many ways, China is meeting Angola's short-term reconstruction and development needs, with seemingly no strings attached.

Plenty of money – no interference in domestic affairs

China was not the Angolan government's first choice for external strategic partnership after the war, as its preference lay with the Western countries. However, as outlined above, the West rebuffed Angola's best efforts to seek post-conflict reconstruction support, demanding that assistance be tied to greater transparency and accountability in Angola's management of substantial inflows of oil revenues. A debilitated regime that had staked considerable political capital on the promise of a post-conflict economic boom could not afford to meet Western demands for several reasons. First, this would have delayed the launch of the post-conflict reconstruction programme, thus jeopardising peace and security, because the government would have lacked the necessary capital to finance it. Second, the MPLA leadership, as good students of Soviet history, understood the perils of openness and transparency in a society undergoing a series of concurrent transitions, which included moving from a one-party system to a multi-party democracy; from centralised planning to a market economy; from a controlled press to a free press; and from tense state–church relations to expanded religious freedoms. In sum, it involved moving from a closed to an open society. Third, the regime was corrupt and its ruling members had no interest in financing the reconstruction programme with the considerable resources they had extracted from the state during decades of conflict.

The West's rebuff forced the Angolan government into what turned out to be the ideal partnership for this specific phase of post-conflict reconstruction. China was in a position to provide what the West could not – cheap money and even cheaper labour – in exchange for oil. China made no demands that could be construed as interference in its internal affairs, which was equally important for Angola.

China's calculated indifference to other countries' internal affairs can partly be explained in relation to its own democratic and human rights deficits. However, this posture is mainly a reflection of the hyper mercantilism triggered by the 'going out' dimension of China's overall development strategy for the first two decades of this century. Jiang Zemin's (2002) guidance for China to seize the opportunities presented by 'the new situation of economic globalisation' was straightforward: 'bring into play our comparative advantages, consolidate our existing markets and open new ones in an effort to increase exports.' Angola represented more to China than a new market for its exports. It was equally significant that Angola was soon to become China's main supplier of crude oil (*Economist* 2010), in exchange for loans to finance urgently needed post-conflict reconstruction projects, especially transportation infrastructure, to re-establish both economic activity and the state's reach throughout the country. As noted above, China is also playing a critical role in revitalising other key sectors and, as a result, is helping the regime to achieve important short-term political goals. But given the complexities of the post-conflict reconstruction and development tasks, it is unlikely that even such a well-endowed partner as China can resolve most of Angola's many challenges.

Angola–China relations: the issue of sustainability

The civil war destroyed the country and delayed the realisation of most citizens' post-colonial aspirations. Thus, the end of the war presented the government with two main challenges: how to rebuild the country and how to enable citizens to fulfil their aspirations. Failure to meet either of these could produce unsustainable political challenges for the regime in the sense that it would open the government to charges of incompetence. In other words, the MPLA government had little choice but to initiate an ambitious national infrastructure (re)building process. Several commentators have focused on the scope and speed of this process (Marques de Morais 2011, Corkin 2011).

Although the impressive nature of the effort taking place in Angola today cannot be doubted, managing it poses important challenges and creates irritants for Angola–China relations. The main challenge revolves around the fact that the structural disequilibria that evolved since independence cannot be quickly rectified by the current (re)building programme. In some cases, especially housing, the pace of (re)building is not nearly fast enough to meet existing and growing demand. The demand for housing (and other basic needs, for that matter) is so high that even with massive assistance from China and current break-neck growth rates in the sector it will not be fully dealt with for another generation or more.

In other cases, however, the government is unable to keep pace with the Chinese juggernaut: many school buildings remain empty because there are not enough teachers while clinics are not used because of lack of doctors and nurses. Even more problematically, some of the recently built roads, hospitals, and stadia are falling into disrepair due to lack of trained maintenance workers. Also, importantly, the Angolan government will have to create the conditions for fast employment growth to enable citizens to afford whatever goods and services a growing economy provides. Although the Angolan government views China as a strategic ally, the common citizen is understandably more preoccupied with immediate rewards, or the lack of them, from the economic boom brought about by the Chinese presence. As Chinese companies meet their labour demands with Chinese workers, only a negligible number of Angolans are able to find jobs on the many construction sites that abound throughout the country. There is also resentment resulting from Angolan entrepreneurs being crowded out by Chinese businesspeople who have competed aggressively for space in the service sector (Redvers 2011).

These twin issues – inability to satisfy pent-up demand and slow job creation – pose serious political problems for the Angolan government. If past performance provides any indication, the Angolan government will continue to be averse to taking responsibility for its problems so as not to damage its legitimacy. This poses a potential source of irritation inasmuch as the Angolan government may encourage the development of a popular perception that views China as mainly responsible for any problems – both in terms of quantity and quality – that may arise in the implementation of the reconstruction programme. Already, whenever quality issues arise, China is viewed as the main culprit. Two such instances are worth noting for illustrative purposes. In 2010, Chinese companies built several stadia to enable Angola to host the African Nations Cup soccer tournament. News reports emerged soon after the tournament ended indicating that some of the stadia had developed cracks due to poor maintenance. Insinuations about Chinese companies' cavalier attitude to quality were strongly rejected by the Chinese ambassador in Luanda, who pointed the finger at Angola's lack of capacity to look after completed projects. In June 2010, patients had to be evacuated from a brand-new Chinese-built hospital in Luanda after large cracks developed in the structure. As the Sino-Angolan relationship evolves, more such episodes are expected to occur.

Conclusion

Although Angola has had few successes in its 35 years of independence, foreign relations are clearly the exception. Persistent diplomatic efforts by the Angolan government to solve the daunting domestic challenges it inherited at independence have yielded important results, including ending the civil war in 2002. The government's ultimate victory on the battlefield is only partly attributable to the military prowess of its armed forces and the UNITA rebels' propensity to overplay their strategic and tactical advantages. Above all, success in foreign relations can be attributed to MPLA's recognition of the inextricable connection between Angola's domestic security and foreign relations. At independence, MPLA recognised that its survival involved thwarting its neighbours' hostile intentions. Given its lack of resources, the MPLA leadership engaged international friends and secured their assistance to this end.

When the process of regime consolidation was threatened in the 1980s because of resurgent rebel military activity and rising regional and international pressure in the form of increased financial military assistance for the rebels, the Angolan government's diplomatic efforts ensured that it once again secured sufficient external support to ensure survival. In the 1990s, internal and external threats were magnified following the collapse of Angola's main external backer, the Soviet Union. Against the odds, Angola's often-unconventional diplomacy, which involved developing an intricate network during the 1990s for procuring arms on the international black market to circumvent a stiff arms embargo, ensured that it prevailed over the rebels.

It is equally significant that Angola responded to its post-conflict internal challenges of reconstruction by looking abroad. When Western countries did not respond to its pleas for financial assistance, Angola shifted its diplomatic attention eastward and succeeded in developing an important strategic partnership with China. Through persistence and constant recalibration, Angola's foreign relations have enabled the regime to survive. Challenges remain, however, especially at the domestic level. Democratic transition and the challenges of transparent governance will dominate Angolan politics for the foreseeable future. They are likely to become even more complicated when long-time president José Eduardo dos Santos leaves the stage. Angola's foreign relations will again play a critical role in meeting the looming challenges. This time, the focus will be on wooing the United States and other mature democracies to complement the assistance currently provided by China and to help Angola stay on course as it moves towards positive peace.

Notes

1. Banco Nacional de Angola.
2. GRAE – Governo Revolucionário de Angola no Exílio.
3. Soon after Savimbi left GRAE in 1964, he led a group of his top lieutenants to China for military training at the prestigious Nanjing Military Academy. Savimbi formally created UNITA in 1966 and continued to draw inspiration, if not consistent support, from China for much of his remaining anti-colonial struggle.
4. This was owing to Zairean backing.

References

Corkin, L. (2011) 'Uneasy allies: China's evolving relations with Angola' *Journal of Contemporary African Studies*, 29(2): 169–80

Economist (2010) 'Rising Angola: oil, glorious oil', 28 January, http://www.economist.com/node/15401935, accessed 4 March 2012

Human Rights Watch (2010) *Transparency and Accountability in Angola*, 13 April, http://www.hrw.org/en/reports/2010/04/13/transparency-and-accountability-angola, accessed 4 March 2012

Konings, P. (2007) 'China and Africa: building a strategic partnership.' *Journal of Developing Societies*, 23: 341–67

Kurlantzick, J. (2006) 'Beijing's safari: China's move into Africa and its implications for aid, development, and governance', *Policy Outlook*, Washington, DC, Carnegie Endowment for International Peace

Malaquias, A. (2011) 'Angola's foreign policy: pragmatic recalibrations', *SAIIA Occasional Paper*, 84

Marques de Morais, R. (2011) 'The new imperialism: China in Angola', *World Affairs*, 173(6): 67–74

Obiorah, N. (2008) 'Rise and rights in China–Africa relations', *SAIS Working Papers in African Studies*, Washington, DC, Johns Hopkins University

Pawson, L. (2011) 'Angola is stirred by the spirit of revolution', *Guardian*, 8 March, http://www.guardian.co.uk/commentisfree/2011/mar/08/angola-spirit-revolution, accessed 4 March 2012

Pei, M. (2008) *China's Trapped Transition: The Limits of Developmental Autocracy*, Cambridge, Harvard University Press

Redvers, L. (2011) 'Cracks show in China's Angola partnership', *Asia Times Online*, 9 February, http://atimes.com/atimes/China_Business/MB09Cb01.html, accessed 4 March 2012

Xinhua (2010) 'China, Angola, establish strategic partnership', *People's Daily Online*, 21 November, http://english.people.com.cn/90001/90776/90883/7205628.html, accessed 4 March 2012

Zemin, J. (2002) 'Build a well-off society in an all-round way and create a new situation in building socialism with Chinese characteristics', speech delivered to the 16th Communist Party of China Congress, 8 November, http://english.people.com.cn/features/16thpartyreport/home.html, accessed 4 March 2012

3

Angolan political elites' management of Chinese credit lines

Lucy Corkin

China Exim Bank's entry into Angola

China supported most of Angola's liberation movements prior to independence in 1975, but Beijing chose to support Savimbi's União Nacional Para a Independência Total de Angola (UNITA) against Soviet-backed Movimento Popular para a Libertação de Angola during Angola's civil war (Taylor 2006: 81). Snow (1988: 77), however, draws attention to the fact that despite China's infamy in supporting UNITA, the MPLA's first crucial, albeit limited, funding came from China.[1] It is this fact that allows Chinese and Angolan officials to gloss over China's rather inconvenient support of the Angolan incumbent regime's mortal enemy, UNITA, over a period of time. Politicians from both countries also liberally refer to a 'long history of relations' between the two countries, despite the fact that Angola's official bilateral contact with China has not been as extensive as that of other African states.[2] Official relations were established between China and Angola in January 1983. With characteristic pragmatism, former ideological paradigms have been discarded by both governments in order to pursue increasingly commercially driven relations. Indeed, the ruling party now has strong ties to Beijing due to China Exim Bank's and several other Chinese financial institutions' sizeable loans to the Angolan government.

Negotiations for financing from China for the Angola Public Investments Programme (PIP) began after the end of the civil war in 2002. This culminated in the signing of a framework agreement on 26 November 2003 between the Chinese ministry of commerce and Angola's ministry of finance (ERA 2009: 81).[3] In February 2005, Vice Premier Zeng Peiyan made a state visit to Angola, during which time the first loan agreement amounting to $2 billion with China Exim Bank was announced. By September 2007, the loan amount had been extended by an additional $2.5 billion (Gabinet de Apoio Técnico 2007: 2). In July 2010, the Angolan minister of finance confirmed that negotiations were underway to finalise a further $6 billion from China Exim Bank to assist with Angola's reconstruction,[4] bringing China Exim Bank total pledged loans to $10.5 billion.[5]

The loan is repayable at three-month Libor[6] plus 1.5 per cent over 17 years, including a grace period of five years.[7] According to Alves (2010: 12) the interest was reduced to Libor plus 1.25 per cent for further tranches following the initial $4.5 billion loan. China Exim Bank's lending policy is to structure a loan so that there is a revenue stream that will be able to support the debt repayment.[8] Through the framework agreement signed with China (represented by the ministry of commerce), the Angolan government, through Sonangol, sells the oil extracted from its concessions to China. The agreement is to supply China with a fixed amount of oil on a quarterly basis. In the case of Angola, the oil shipments are priced according to the international spot price of the day.[9] The loans extended by China Exim Bank are targeted specifically towards facilitating public investment in Angola and are officially managed by the Angolan ministry of finance (Burke and Corkin 2006; Vines et al 2009). The Angolan political elite, primarily the presidency, has seized the opportunities presented by engagement with China to strengthen and reinforce mechanisms through which it retains power. This paper discusses the role of the Angolan political elite in shaping the process and outcome of the China Exim Bank credit lines. These actions are further placed in the context of the Angolan government's own ambitions in an international, regional and domestic context.

'Angolanisation' of the China Exim Bank loan

The mechanism of the loan disbursement is specifically structured so that China Exim Bank retains control of the disbursements and pays the Chinese companies that have undertaken the projects directly so as to isolate the loans from the risks of the Angolan banking system. Brautigam (2010) refers to this as an 'agency of restraint'. However, the financing from Beijing has not remained completely immune from corruption. In late 2004, finance minister José Pedro de Morais was summoned to Beijing to answer to allegations of misappropriation of Exim Bank funding (Ferreira 2008: 297). In an attempt to reform reporting structures, the Gabinete de Apoio Técnico (GAT)[10] was established in September 2004 at the ministry of finance, which reported to an 'Inter-Sector Monitoring Commission' led by the minister of finance, José Pedro de Morais; the minister of public works, Higenio Carneiro; the Banco Nacional de Angola (BNA) governor, Amadeu Maurício; the secretary to the council of ministers, António van Dúnem, and the CEO of Sonangol, Manuel Vicente (ERA 2009: 82). In October 2004, ostensibly to further mitigate problems with corruption, President Eduardo dos Santos and Prime Minister Fernando Piedade Dias dos Santos, in consultation with the Chinese government, established the Gabinete de Reconstrução Nacional (GRN), headed by General 'Kopelipa' Hélder Vieira Dias, who is also minister of the Casa Militár.[11]

Thus, whereas the ministry of finance is the state organ with which China Exim Bank has signed the official agreements, GRN retains a parallel function, allowing the president to achieve direct access to the credit lines. Given that GRN is headed by the highest military authority in the land, access is difficult as information regarding GRN falls under the jurisdiction of state security organs. This seemingly all-encompassing power of GRN scuttled any attempts at accountability as this organ reports directly to the presidency, under one of his closest associates.

In mid-2010, GRN's power was reportedly removed. Marques de Morais (2011: 73) suggested General Kopelipa was under investigation for the way that the previous credit lines had been managed. State-owned newspaper *Jornal de Angola* (2010a) reported in May 2010 that President dos Santos had appointed as director of GRN Antonio Texeira Flor, a former vice minister of urbanism and housing. This restructuring may indeed have been due to accusations of mismanagement of funds or in order to reduce the power of General Kopelipa, who had previously had unfettered access to Chinese funds as former head of GRN.[12] An Angolan activist remarked that GRN was to all intents and purposes 'finished' as its former mandate was being handed to Sonangol.[13] Indeed, *Jornal de Angola* (2010b) quoted the president confirming as much, with most responsibilities being transferred to the newly formed Sonangol Imobiliária (Sonangol Real Estate),[14] and 'other entities'.

Even though GRN has been dismantled, the transfer of its powers to Sonangol is hardly an improvement on transparency and accountability.[15] The parastatal has long had a reputation as an 'island of competence' (Soares de Oliveira 2007a: 595) amid Angola's inefficient bureaucracies, but is also almost a parallel treasury, with little accountability other than to the president (Hodges 2003; Soares de Oliveira 2007a, 2007b; Shaxson 2007: 51). The oil company, despite having been in existence since 1976, published its first externally audited accounts in mid-2010. Global Witness (2011: 5) has found a $8.55 billion difference in the reported figures for oil revenue between Sonangol and the ministries of finance and petroleum; the accounts of the ministries also appear not to match.

Parallel structures of Chinese financing

What is perhaps unique in Angola's situation is the presence of another seemingly parallel and unrelated financing structure directed from China to Angola whose links to the Chinese government appear ill-defined.[16] From 2005, credit lines from China International Fund Ltd (CIF), a Hong Kong-based company established in 2003, have also been placed under the auspices of GRN.

The loans managed by GRN, implicitly assumed to be financing from CIF, were estimated to be approximately $9.8 billion within a year of the office's establishment.[17] However, the controversy surrounding these loans prompted the Angolan ministry of finance to issue its first ever official press release regarding the various Chinese credit lines. The Ministry of Finance (2007) clarified that CIF, described as a 'private institution', had been created for the following purpose:

- Creating facilities or credit lines to finance projects within the framework of the national reconstruction office
- Obtaining new funds on more competitive terms
- Promoting national and international venture-capital investment in Angola.

The same press release reported that CIF had made available financing amounting to the smaller amount of $2.9 billion. These funds were earmarked to carry out various construction projects such as the building of a new international airport in Luanda, road and railway rehabilitation as well as drainage in Luanda city. Due to difficulties in securing financing, the Angolan government instructed the Angolan ministry of finance to secure domestic funding through the sale of treasury bonds to the value of $3.5 billion (Angolan Ministry of Finance 2007).

CIF appears to be a private institution through which private Chinese clients can channel investments into Africa and beyond. Increasingly known for its opacity, CIF has generated considerable international controversy following the announcement of less-than-transparent loan agreements in Latin America (Levkowitz et al 2009) and Guinea (*Africa–Asia Confidential* 2009). It was also related to a highly publicised case of insider trading on the Shanghai stock market.[18] Vines, Wong, Weimer and Campos (2009: 51) have also pointed to the importance of the CIF directors' connections with both Chinese and Angolan officials in securing prominent contracts in Angola.

The Chinese government has distanced itself from CIF. One respondent explained that the Chinese government has mandated all the state-owned companies not to help CIF in undertaking their projects. Indeed, the Chinese government through its state-owned banks would reportedly like to assume ownership of the projects CIF currently manages.[19] They appear to be doing so, which may mean that they may have assumed CIF's debt as well. CITIC Construction, a Chinese state-owned enterprise (SOE) has assumed the management of a large-scale housing project in the Kilamba Kiaxi district outside of Luanda.[20]

Several Chinese respondents commented on the important and yet harmful (to Chinese government interests) role that CIF is playing in Angola. It is acknowledged that CIF must have high-level access to the Angolan government and operates under the consent of the Angolan president, and with possible former links to the Chinese government, although all were adamant that CIF is a private entity.[21] According to Marques de Morais (2011: 71) a Chinese official is reported to have said of them: 'CIF is a company that has no construction record or credentials... Largely they are brokers who get contracts from the Angolan government and sell them to other Chinese companies for huge profits.' However, this describes the role of any main contractor in the construction industry and is hardly sinister in and of itself.[22] What is clear is that the reporting lines, described as the official lines of communication with regards to the Chinese financing in Angola, have been blurred and subverted considerably by well-connected political figures.

The oil intermediary

CIF's role in the China Exim Bank mechanism takes on considerable significance in terms of the oil sales to China used as repayment for the credit lines. The oil is transferred by China Angola Oil Stock Holding, a subsidiary of Beiya (now Dayuan) International Development, the same parent company of CIF (Alden and Alves 2009: 13) and with connections to China Sonangol[23] (Vines et al 2009: 50). Similarly, according to its website, China Sonangol is also engaged in exporting oil from Angola to China as part of its portfolio of business activities.[24]

This situation is not condoned by the Chinese government, which would rather receive the oil directly in repayment for the loans.[25] As explained by one respondent, CIF profits considerably from its role as intermediary. Some of the profits go towards the financing of CIF's projects in Angola.[26] Indeed, he further intimated that the Angolan president himself was profiting through the intermediary firm. He suggested that this corruption was reducing developmental benefits that Angola could attain through oil cooperation with the Chinese state directly. Perhaps corroborating this, Vines et al (2011: 4) quote reports suggesting that President dos Santos's son, José Filomeno 'Zenu' dos Santos, is China Sonangol's official representative.

Elite subversion of the China Exim Bank credit line

President dos Santos is adept at juggling the institutions tasked with managing national reconstruction. In the case of the Chinese financing, it is clear that the establishment of GRN under a close presidential associate was designed to balance the growing clout of the ministry of finance under José Pedro de Morais, which originally managed the China Exim Bank loans. The parallel structures have made it difficult to coordinate the process, reducing the efficacy of both as centres of power as they act as counterweights to one another. This is described by Migdal (1988: 211) as a classic strategy employed by leaders seeking to weaken any state apparatus that might threaten their own power.

With the same objective, the president is also adept at reshuffling key positions in order to prevent the institutionalisation of figures in places of power. Access to the Chinese credit lines, as discussed, is nominally managed by the ministry of finance but is closely monitored by the president. The president has been quick to reshuffle the line of command if any political figures are suspected of gaining too much influence by their proximity to the credit lines, ensuring that he is the sole source of political continuity. The power to be able to enact such bureaucratic changes rests with the president's powers of appointment, enshrined in the 2010 constitution, which extend to all high-level positions in government as well as the judiciary.[27] The frequency with which dos Santos exercises these powers shows that they are also often employed to identify a scapegoat for political issues[28] while simultaneously distancing the president, despite the fact that most national policies require executive approval.[29]

Essentially, this situation serves to ensure the weakness of potentially powerful state agencies that might threaten the power of the presidency (Migdal 1988: 213). This thesis is supported by van de Walle (2001: 127) who further describes the neo-patrimonial state as a 'hybrid regime' with a parallel structure of informal institutions within the formation of the state. He asserts that this serves the purpose of undermining a bureaucracy that might otherwise serve as a restraining influence on elite power. In the case of Angola, such informal networks provide a channel through which the resultant inefficient bureaucracy can be circumvented should the need arise. This produces a further centralisation of power around the presidency to whom these channels inevitably report. It also distances the president from the bureaucratic inefficiency of his own creation (Comerford 2005: 110). As noted by Reno (2000: 231–2) 'the Angolan government shows a great capacity … to manipulate the conditions of their own bureaucratic weakness.'

The Angolan elite in general and the presidency in particular have accrued significant benefits from the credit lines in several ways. On a very literal level, the Chinese credit line represents a new source of economic rents, centrally controlled by the presidency in order to preserve political dominance as the gatekeeper to such wealth. The president in particular, however, has managed to instrumentalise the credit lines for a wider set of objectives and has managed to subvert the China Exim Bank loan process in order to consolidate and retain both economic and political power.

Balancing international relations

Accepting loans from China was politically expedient for the Angolan political elite for several reasons. Firstly, Angola had been experiencing difficulties securing other sources of capital on conditions acceptable to the dos Santos regime. The Angolan government has developed a strong narrative variously directed at both domestic and international audiences. Of central importance, given the relationship with China, is the story of rejection and abandonment by the international community following the end of the civil war. A planned conference of donors to drum up support for reconstruction did not materialise, despite the government having 'used all their diplomatic means' to try to get this result. This was a bitter pill for the government; it seems, as it was believed that, due to their involvement, the international community would have a 'moral obligation for them to help us reconstruct'.[30]

Interestingly, this is believed across all sectors of Angolan society and by international observers as well.[31] One Angolan civil society advocate voiced the belief that Angola had been thrust into the arms of China due to the West's abandonment of Angola 'demanding things that were completely unacceptable'.[32] China was seen as the logical development partner when assistance was not forthcoming elsewhere.

Particularly in the last few years, on the back of a strong oil price and Angola's debt normalisation, Luanda has been approved an increasing number of credit lines from a number of countries. Aside from the material assistance that China's Exim Bank loans has provided, the provision of funds seems to have acted in part as a kind of financial catalyst for other flows of financing.[33]

Spain alone in 2007 provided $600 million in construction aid (Angop 2007). Furthermore Canada's Export Development Bank has signed an agreement with Angola's Banco de Poupança e Crédito for $1 billion in 2008 to finance government infrastructure projects and $16 million for private enterprise projects. Brazil's Banco Nacional de Desenvolvimento Económico e Social (BNDES) disbursed $1.5 billion to fund the purchase of Brazilian construction equipment in Angola in the first five months of 2009 and further offered $250 million to fund projects in Angola. Angola has recently attracted the interest of other financiers, most notably the World Bank, which is extending loans of $1 billion from 2009 to 2013 to assist with the African country's economic diversification. Credit lines from European countries, while forthcoming, are not comparable in size to those of China. For comparison, in the first half of 2009 Germany extended $1.7 billion to Angola, Portugal $500 million (Macauhub 2009), US Exim Bank offered $120 million and Britain $70 million in credit.

An agreement was also put in place for the Angolan government to service its Paris Club debt. The bulk of the $2.3 billion had been paid by December 2007, and plans were made to service the $1.8 billion in interest accrued during the civil war (Kiala 2010: 324).

Such developments led to a considerable thawing of relations between Angola and the international financial institutions. Recall that in 2002, negotiations with the IMF had collapsed over the loans' conditionalities, leading Angola to turn to China for financing. In November 2009, the IMF made provisions for a standby loan of $1.4 billion for Angola, 300 per cent of Angola's drawing quota. Indeed, far from alienating financial institutions such as the IMF and the World Bank as some have claimed (Soares de Oliveira 2007b: 295), one could argue that Angola has actively courted them, in order to balance China's influence in the country.

Angola, despite international concerns, particularly in the context of strengthening China–Angola relations, will strongly resist becoming or being perceived as a client state of any other country and will continue to engage with all international actors. Indeed, Martins (2010: 1) describes Angola as having a 'multi-vector' foreign policy, managing 'to keep a balance of interests regarding foreign intervention in its domestic markets'. Angola is also distinct from most oil states as encouraging Western business rather than fostering anti-Western sentiment.[34] The China Exim Bank credit lines have thus been successfully managed in order to solicit further financing from other foreign partners, while simultaneously balancing the influence of Chinese financing in the Angolan economy.

State infrastructure provision and the 2008 elections

Chinese funding has also allowed the Angolan government to initiate a series of prestige projects which may have a tenuous link to development, but have been important in galvanising the regime's image domestically and internationally.[35] Angola hosted the 'Afrobasket' African basketball Championships in 2007 (which it won) and the African Cup of Nations in 2009. Although this was very much directed at an external projection of the country's rising prestige, it was also important for domestic constituencies, given the universal popularity of football (Almeida 2009).

Some of the infrastructure projects have had genuine developmental benefits for Angolan citizens. With an eye on the inevitability of national elections, which took place in 2008, the ruling party saw the political dividends of public investment in infrastructure.[36] Many of the works, planned for completion just prior to the elections, were presented as MPLA achievements, rather than government achievements, blurring the distinction between the party and the state. This calculated merging of ruling party and state institutions allowed the MPLA to benefit from the successful delivery of such public works. They were arguably particularly important in rural areas where infrastructure was not only sorely needed, but the MPLA image required bolstering.

The MPLA, Pawson (2008) argues, has thus used its political

dominance to subvert the electoral process of September 2008 in order to gain international sanction for the consolidation of the ruling party's hold on power. This resonates with Messiant's (2007: 106) description of MPLA manipulation of the previous elections in 1992 in what she terms the 'consolidation of hegemonic power'. The 2008 elections, during which MPLA secured 87 per cent of parliamentary seats, provided much-needed legitimacy to MPLA rule, not only for international observers, who declared the ballot 'free and fair' (Orre 2010: 8) but for their domestic constituencies. Furthermore, the landslide parliamentary victory facilitated a new constitution which further consolidates incumbent power, albeit lawfully at a procedural level.[37]

Exclusion of local participation in national reconstruction

National reconstruction has been advanced as an urgent priority by the Angolan government. However, the mechanism through which this is pursued focuses only on the projects themselves as constitutive of the physical rebuilding of the country's infrastructure as this is the part of the process that the presidency can directly control.[38]

According to the terms of the loan, mostly Chinese companies are contracted to undertake the construction projects. It was also negotiated that 30 per cent of contract value was to be allocated to the Angolan private sector to encourage Angolan participation in the reconstruction process (Corkin 2008). Although a minority percentage, it is arguably a realistic condition, given the paucity of skilled labour and local industries to support the material requirements of projects of this scale. Many Angolan construction industry professionals, however, feel that Chinese companies are afforded an unfair advantage due to the policies surrounding the credit lines.[39] The blame for this is laid squarely at the door of the Angolan state. However, there is little evidence to show that local Angolan companies have been able to cope even with their reserved quota. A ministry of finance official confirmed that the 30 per cent quota condition was only upheld if it 'did not compromise project deadlines'.[40] This suggests that while policy concessions are made, little is done to support the nascent industries in practice as they try to fulfil their quota of the contract work.

According to Schmitz (2007: 418) successful industrial policy should challenge enterprises to meet certain criteria set by the government and provide support in order for them to do so. Unfortunately, Angolan local content policies seem to do the former without the latter. Few Angolans in the construction sector feel that they are receiving sufficient support from the government.[41] Furthermore, while the Angolan government does make it increasingly difficult to bring in foreign labour, there are as yet no viable local alternatives. As a result, it appears that Angolanisation policies are patchily enforced in order not to halt the industry completely. Thus, despite a body of local content laws, there are several notable examples of the contradicting policy environment present in Angola, whereby short-term gain is prioritised above local content development.

The Angolan government has in theory put in place a robust set of local content laws, yet rarely oversees their effective implementation. It is also apparent that there is a lack of interaction between Chinese companies and local policy formulation. One government researcher suggested that 'the African countries need to ... create a better environment for employment',[42] another that there have been 'half efforts', but not much effort on this front and that there needs to be cooperation with the African side to make the deal more realistic.[43] From the Angolan government's side, however, it appears that the political will necessary to enforce policies related to local content and skills transfer is not yet adequate. As commented by a Western construction contractor: 'What is absent in Angola is the emphasis on local employment and skills development. An infrastructure project should be a vehicle for social development. This mentality is totally absent here.'[44]

The Angolan government has not focused on rebuilding 'soft' infrastructure, such as concurrent institution- and capacity-building through local participation. While the official reason is that such processes slow projects' completion schedules, it could be argued the real reason is that political elites have a vested interest in retaining a monopoly over existing economic activity and preventing the formation of what Migdal (1988: 211) terms 'power centres'. This prevents the potential rise of independent entrepreneurs operating outside of their own patronage networks (Bayart 1993: 91).[45] In the balancing act between political stability and economic growth referred to by Migdal (1988: 236), it appears that (short-term) political stability prevails. The contradictory policy environment ensures that only the politically connected may benefit from the reconstruction process, thus reinforcing the political and economic status quo maintained by patronage networks.[46] In this way, the political elite has adapted the patronage system to serve in peace time, or instrumentalised the post-war environment, as suggested by De Beer and Gamba (2000); or, as described by Soares de Oliveira (2007a: 148), has 'adapted its grip to a peace-time gear'. *CHINA'S Infrastructure Rules*

An Angolan activist pointed out the lack of long-term strategic priorities: 'there are no incentives in the economy with the result that cement, "mosaic", basic construction material, steel, must all come from China. There are actually incentives to import, so local industries could not compete in a market economy.'[47] Practically, this means that not only is the rhetoric not in alignment with the policy, but it may indeed be in the elite's interests for implementation not to be successful. As one Angolan activist pointed out, short-lived projects[48] that continually need to be repaired ensure a continuing stream of construction contracts and the potential for rents.[49]

Furthermore, the lack of participation by Angolan society means that the implementation and process of the construction projects is not rendering as much benefit to local industries as it might. It is rather seen as the provision of an end product. Marques de Morais (2011: 71) argues that:

> 'It [the Chinese role] has enabled a string of political measures aimed at perpetuating the power of the president's inner circle, while setting back internal dialogue on national reconstruction even within the ruling party itself. The Chinese presence has also spawned a mass fantasy about national goals that bears no resemblance to what can really be accomplished — the sheer weight of which, along with threats of repression, often silences critics of the Dos Santos regime.'

Marques de Morais (2010a, 2010b, 2010c) has published extensively on the move from Marxism-Leninism to capitalism as a strategy through which political elites could effectively privatise state assets at substantial profit to themselves. He has expanded this to the Chinese credit line – viewing it as a new avenue for elite enrichment under the guise of national reconstruction. He comments (2011: 73):

> Angola is run through an extensive fabric of patronage networks enhanced by the fact that ninety-five per cent of the country's export revenues, which are essential for patronage, derive from foreign-controlled offshore oil production. Such economic arrangements have insulated the Dos Santos regime from the will of the Angolan people, who remain economically and politically irrelevant. China's new prominence is part of an effort by the ruling elite to keep them that way by excluding society at large from the task of national reconstruction.

In a bid to increase the role Angolan society and businesses can play in the national reconstruction programme, the current minister of the economy, Abraão Gourgel, announced during the visit to Luanda of vice-premier Xi Jinping that it was necessary to introduce 'adjustments' to Angola's cooperation with China, in order to increase the benefits accrued to Angolan companies (*Journal de Angola*, 2010d). While these are indeed the correct noises that need to be heard, the pronouncements were characteristically vague. This relates to the Angolan government's political will and capacity to follow on to the implementation of their successfully negotiated agreement with China Exim Bank.

Conclusion

Angola's relationship with China, it seems, has matured from a heady embrace of mutual convenience to a reassessment of each other's strategic significance as partners. Indeed, relations with China seem to have formed part of a successful strategy employed to bolster regime stability domestically and boost Angolan government standing internationally. Hearty political posturing indicates that both China and Angola see each other as necessary strategic allies for the foreseeable future, but this may mask an uneasy marriage of convenience. A Chinese respondent commented that relations were not as good as widely assumed. In his opinion, dos Santos has not come to China very many times, despite the considerable assistance that China has given Angola in the form of infrastructure.[50]

While it could be argued that the government is seeking to rebuild the country in the quickest and most cost effective way (i.e. through Chinese contractors), it is clear that some sectors of the population are being alienated by the approach as not enough is being done to include them in the process, thus foregoing the long-term benefits of nation building. Indeed, the result is state building through consolidation of the MPLA's political and economic hegemony in the country. In fact it could be viewed that the provision of public goods is being 'outsourced' and privatised, where arguably the role of the state in this context should be to nurture the growth of local development and nascent indigenous industries, particularly during national reconstruction.

Chinese commentators have pointed out that the onus is not on China to develop Africa; rather this is the responsibility of African governments themselves.[51] Given the ease with which the Futungo[52] has incorporated Chinese funding into the consolidation of domestic political power, it is unlikely that Angola's development or lack thereof is a result of genuine lack of capacity. It is far more likely that it is due to a lack of political will and institutions weakened by design. Moreover, I argue that the lack of support for broader-based local participation in the national reconstruction process is a conscious strategy to prevent the creation of economic growth independent of the patronage linkages of the political elite. This is to deter political challenges to the ruling party's control from an alternative economic base of power.

Clearly, there is a mismatch between professed policy goals and practical implementation, illustrating that while the Angolan government is using the China Exim Bank loan-financed projects to fortify its discourse of national reconstruction, the lack of follow-through on policies suggests a distinct lack of political will to engender broad-based economic empowerment.

In Angola's case external relations have been the political elite's source of power since their assumption of government. In the realm of external relations, it is useful to recall Bayart's (1993: 74) concept of 'extroversion', whereby the monopoly of access to foreign influence and capital is used as an additional tool to maintain power. Both van de Walle (2001) and Chabal (2007) point to the fact that the manipulation by Angolan political parties of such external actors is routinely underestimated, once again denying the role of African agency in prolonging the conflict in order to accrue economic benefits. This raises the thesis proposed by Clapham (2008: 366) that China will merely become the next in a long line of actors to be channelled by African elites for their own political agendas.

Notes

1. The first contact between MPLA and the Communist Party of China (CPC) was at the Conference of the Afro-Asian Peoples' Solidarity Organisation (APSO) held in Guinea Conakry in April 1960. Following an invitation from the CPC, Mario Pinto de Andrade, the MPLA president, Viriato da Cruz, secretary general, and Lúcio Lara visited China later in 1960. They brought back crucial funding for the nascent independence movement. The MPLA leadership actually experienced a schism as to whether to ally with Soviet Russia or Communist China. Viriato da Cruz, one of the founding fathers of MPLA, was ousted as a result of the decision to follow Moscow. He fled to Beijing, where he died in exile in 1973 (Pinto de Andrade 2007: 3). It is suspected that the liberation movement turned to the USSR in order to access more advanced weapons technology than those available from China.
2. This does not mean that interaction did not occur before official diplomatic ties were established, however. China had extensive involvement in Angola's civil war.
3. This source actually refers to an agreement between the Angolan ministry of finance and China's ministry of foreign trade and economic cooperation (MOFTEC), but MOFTEC was restructured to become the Chinese ministry of commerce (MOFCOM) in March 2003, eight months previously.
4. Angolan minister of finance, Carlos Albert Lopes, broadcast on Radio Nacional de Angola, 4pm, 9 July 2010. This deal was mentioned as having been signed in November 2009 by a respondent from China Exim Bank (Interview, deputy general manager at one of the finance departments at China Exim Bank, Beijing, 9 December 2009).
5. In fact the signing of the additional $6 billion loan was confirmed by an informed source at China Exim Bank eight months previously (Interview, deputy general manager at one of the finance departments of China Exim Bank, Beijing, 9 December 2009).
6. Interest rate is quoted according to the Angolan ministry of finance. Libor, according to the British Banker's Association, is the most widely used benchmark or reference rate for short term interest rates.
7. Interview, GAT, Angolan ministry of finance, Luanda, 30 May 2007.
8. Interview, Philip Karp, regional coordinator for East Asia and Pacific, World Bank Institution, Beijing, 14 October 2009.
9. Interview, department general manager, China Exim Bank, Beijing, 9 December 2009.

10. Technical support office.
11. The visit of the President of China Exim Bank at the time, Yang Zilin, in September 2004 was reportedly in order to resolve issues of embezzlement related to the China Exim Bank credit line (ERA, 2009: 82).
12. One respondent mentioned that: 'the legacy is questionable for some; some want the decision to scrap it.' (Interview, senior researcher, private think tank, Luanda, 13 May 2010). Possibly related is the fact that a former high-ranking general, Fernando Garcia Miala, reportedly threatened to identify senior Angolan government officials profiting from diverted Chinese credit line funds (Human Rights Watch 2010). This was allegedly part of a power struggle between the two generals (*Africa–Asia Confidential* 2007). Miala was sentenced to four years' imprisonment for 'insubordination'. Of interest is the fact that in the month immediately after Miala's sentencing on 20 September 2007, the ministry of finance issued a press release with the purpose of 'clarifying' the Chinese credit lines (Angolan Ministry of Finance, 2007). This is the only time the Angolan government has released an official government statement in this regard. Furthermore, Miala only served two years of his sentence, and was released on 9 October 2009 following a presidential pardon in April of that year (HRW 2010).
13. Interview, Angolan anti-corruption activist, Luanda, 2 February 2011.
14. Sonangol Imobiliária, according to a report by *Novo Jornal* (2010) was created as a subsidiary of Sonangol designed to amalgamate the responsibilities of the Cashew Cooperative (Cooperativa Cajueira) and the Engineering Directorate (DENG), previously responsible for constructions undertaken by Sonangol. The director of DENG, Orlando Veloso, was mooted to assume directorship of Sonangol Imobiliária. *Jornal de Angola* (2010c) confirmed that by November 2010 Veloso was the president of the administrative council of Sonangol Imobiliária. The company reportedly owns a 20 per cent share in Mota-Engil Angola (Vines et al 2011: 4). According to the Angolan Ministry of Petroleum (2010: 77) the company manages civil construction projects undertaken by Sonangol and in 2009 managed $208 million of investment, twice the amount initially expected for that year.
15. For an in-depth discussion of the level of transparency and reliability of Sonangol's accounts, see Global Witness (2011).
16. The Chinese government has distanced itself from CIF, but it is likely that CIF has some Chinese government connections (Vines et al 2009: 51; Levkowitz et al 2009: 33).
17. Interview, director of a foreign-invested bank in Luanda, 7 June 2006.
18. In March 2007, previously little-known Hangxiao Steel, a Zhejiang-based Chinese company, announced it had won $4.4 billion in contracts from CIF to sell construction material and services for a public housing project in Angola. Shortly afterwards the China Securities and Regulation Commission (CSRC) undertook to investigate the company, which was listed on the Shanghai stock exchange. Hangxiao's share price had risen

by the maximum of 10 per cent for 10 consecutive days until 16 March; the deal had been announced on 13 March (Kurtenbach 2007). In April CSRC fined the company and five employees, including the chairman and president, a collective RMB 1.1 million ($143,000) for insider trading. The company soon ran into difficulty with the contract. By August 2007 the company had received law suits from 22 investors claiming RMB 2.7 million ($360,000) (*China Daily* 2007).

19. Manager, private Chinese importing business, 15 July 2010.
20. The author visited the construction site of this project. The project is valued at $3.5 billion and encompasses 20,002 residential apartments, 246 commercial units, 24 kindergartens, nine primary schools, eight secondary schools and two electrical substations over 8.8km^2, according to CITIC Construction company information. This may be the project CIF initially awarded to Hangxiao Steel.
21. Interviews: junior researcher, Chinese think tank, Beijing, 16 October 2009; Africa department, Chinese ministry of foreign affairs, Beijing, 29 October 2009; manager, Chinese import company, Luanda, 15 July 2010.
22. Several reports (see for example Vines et al 2009; Levkowitz et al 2009) have questioned the legitimacy and indeed legality of the role of CIF and its related networks of subsidiaries and sister companies in Angola and Africa as a whole. However, despite valid suspicions, nothing of substance has been proven in this regard.
23. China Sonangol is owned by Sonangol (30 per cent) and a private Chinese company called New Bright International Development Ltd (70 per cent). Luo Fanghong, who owns 30 per cent of New Bright International Development, is also chairperson of CIF (Vines et al 2009: 64).
24. http://www.chinasonangol.com/eng/business.asp, accessed 28 April 2011.
25. Manager, private Chinese importing business, Luanda, 15 July 2010.
26. Interview, manager, private Chinese importing business, Luanda, 15 July 2010.
27. Although presidential decrees can be overruled by parliament, in the unlikely event of this occurring, the president can veto parliamentary laws (Orre 2010: 13).
28. An example is the dismissal of housing minister Diekumpuna Sita José in April 2009, as political pressure mounted over an MPLA campaign promise to provide one million houses for the poor.
29. Interestingly, elite advisors are often 'recycled'. Several prominent figures have fallen from grace only to be reinstated or promoted in later years. Examples are Minister of State (civil bureau) Carlos Feijó appointed in 2008, disgraced several years previously, and General Miala, imprisoned for insubordination, but pardoned several years later.
30. Interview, university professor and parliamentarian, Luanda, 18 August 2010.
31. Interview, senior researcher at a private Angolan research institute, Luanda, 13 May 2010.

32. Interview, Luanda, Angolan programme manager, NGO, Luanda, 18 August 2010. This of course refers to the conditions the international financial institutions required prior to releasing funding.
33. Interview, Mr João Manuel Bernardo, Angolan ambassador to Beijing, 28 October 2009.
34. Of course, as pointed out by both Sogge (2009: 8) and Soares de Oliveira (2007b: 52) the nature of Angola's extroverted economy necessitates that Angolan political elites collaborate with Western business interests in order to maintain access to the oil wealth that fuels their patronage networks.
35. An Angola respondent commented: 'The regime is arrogant; they need to be legitimate, to be recognised. There was frustration with the national community in the post-war phase...' (Interview, academic, Luanda, 14 July 2010).
36. MPLA is reported to have taken credit for large-scale infrastructure projects undertaken by the Angolan government in the run-up to the national elections in late 2008.
37. For an in-depth discussion of this, see Orre (2010).
38. Soares de Oliveira describes (2007b:121) the 'privatisation' within oil states whereby the provision of essential services and public goods is effectively outsourced to NGOs or private firms' corporate social responsibility programmes. In the case of national reconstruction, a lack of indigenous human resources and industrial inputs have, it could be argued, necessitated the Angolan state 'outsourcing' the national reconstruction projects' financing and implementation to Chinese companies.
39. José Severino, president, Associação Industrial de Angola (AIA), presentation 'A presença chinesa e o sector privado de Angola', 12 May 2010.
40. Interview, Mr A, technical support department, ministry of finance, Luanda, 6 July 2010.
41. Interview, Mr P, vice president, Angolan industrial organisation, Luanda, 9 July 2010.
42. Interview, Ms W, associate researcher at the Chinese Academy of International Trade and Economic Cooperation (CAITEC), department of aid studies, MOFCOM, 5 December 2009.
43. Interview, Prof L, professor of Africa studies at Beijing-based university, Beijing, 4 January 2010.
44. Interview, Mr G, project director with a Western contractor, Luanda, 6 July 2010.
45. Soares de Oliveira (2007a: 91) details how Sonangol's expansion into non-oil sectors and services has 'crowded out' other entrepreneurs as Sonangol not only commands greater resources, but also demands that international firms form joint ventures with its own subsidiaries, thus making market entry and/or technological transfer opportunities for other fledging Angolan businesses hard to access.

46. This is an example of elites using the market as a policy instrument in order to accrue policy-generated rents (Staniland 1985: 59). As Bayart (1993: 266) notes, 'networks founded on inequality perpetuate inequality'.
47. Interview, Luanda, 18 August 2010.
48. Marques de Morais (2011: 68) comments: 'Throughout the country, tales of the Chinese roads being washed away by rain or filling up with potholes within months of being opened to traffic are now the stuff of legend.'
49. Interview, anti-corruption activist, Luanda, 2 February 2011.
50. Interview, editor in chief, Xinhua, Beijing, 6 December 2009.
51. Victor Yu, managing director, Standard Resources (China) Ltd, presentation at American Chamber of Commerce event 'China Outbound: Investing in Africa and Latin America', Shanghai, 16 September 2009.
52. This is the informal name by which the presidency and its cabal of advisors are known, named for the hill in Luanda from which they operate (Sogge, 2009:14).

References

Africa–Asia Confidential (2007) 'Big oil, high stakes', 2 November
Africa–Asia Confidential (2009) 'Blood and money in the streets: China's business ties to the loathed Câmara junta could quickly backfire', 20 October
Alden, C. and Alves, A.C. (2009) 'China and Africa's natural resources: the challenges and implications for development and governance', *SAIIA Occasional Paper*, 41
Almeida, H. (2009) 'Angola sacks central bank chief – report', 13 April: http://af.reuters.com/article/idAFB11654120090413, accessed 11 April 2012
Alves, A.C. (2010) 'The oil factor in Sino-Angolan relations at the start of the 21st century', *SAIIA Occasional Paper*, 55
Angolan Ministry of Finance (2007) 'Comunicado de imprensa – esclarecimento sobre a linha de crédito da China'
Angolan Ministry of Petroleum (2010) 'Relatório de actividades do sector petrolífero, referente ao ano de 2009'
Angop (2007) 'Country and Spain sign investment protection accord', 21 November 2007
Bayart, J. (1993) *The State of Africa: The Politics of the Belly*, London, Longman Group UK Limited
Brautigam, D. (2010) 'Africa's eastern promise: what the west can learn from Chinese investment in Africa', *Foreign Affairs*, 5 January
Burke, C. and Corkin, L. (2006) 'China's interest and activity in Africa's construction and infrastructure sectors', prepared for the department for international development (DFID), Centre for Chinese Studies, Stellenbosch University
Chabal, P. (2007) 'E Puribus Unum: Transitions in Angola', in Chabal, P. and Vidal, N. (eds) *Angola: The Weight of History*, London, Hurst Publishers

China Daily (2007) 'Question mark over Angola project, says Hangxiao Steel', 7 August

Clapham, C. (2008) 'Fitting China In', in Alden, C., Large, D. and Soares de Oliveira, R. (eds) *China returns to Africa: A Rising Power and a Continent Embrace*, London, Hurst Publishers

Comerford, M.G. (2005) *The Peaceful Face of Angola: Biography of a Peace Process (1991–2002)*, University of Michigan, M. Comerford

Corkin, L. (2008) 'China's interest in Angola's infrastructure and construction sectors', in Guerrero, D.G, and Manji, F. (eds) *China's New Role in Africa and the South*, Oxford, Pambazuka Press

De Beer, H. and Gamba, V. (2000) 'The arms dilemma: resources for arms or arms for resources', in Cilliers, J. and Dietrich, C. (eds) *Angola's War Economy: The Role of Oil and Diamonds*, Pretoria, Institute for Security Studies

Executive Research Associates (ERA) (2009) 'China in Africa: a strategic overview', report prepared for the Institute of Developing Economies, Japan External Trade Organisation, Pretoria

Ferreira, M.E. (2008) 'China and Angola: just a passion for oil?', in Alden, C., Large, D. and Soares de Oliveira, R. (eds) *China Returns to Africa: A Rising Power and a Continent Embrace*, London, Hurst and Company

Gabinet de Apoio Técnico (2007) 'Linha de Crédito com o Eximbank da China: Projectos Concluídos'

Global Witness (2011) *Oil Revenues in Angola: Much More Information, But Not Enough Transparency*, London, Global Witness

Hodges, T. (2003) *Angola: Anatomy of an Oil State*, London, James Currey

Human Rights Watch (HRW) (2010) 'Transparency and accountability in Angola', http://www.hrw.org/sites/default/files/reports/angola0410webwcover_1.pdf, accessed 12 April 2012London, Human Rights Watch

Jornal de Angola (2010a) 'Presidente faz nomeações para o Gabinete de Reconstrução', 29 May

Jornal de Angola (2010b) 'Imobiliária da Sonangol gere novas centralidades', 28 September

Jornal de Angola (2010c) 'PCA da Sonangol Imobiliária visitou reservas fundiárias', 8 November

Jornal de Angola (2010d) 'Angola propõe ajustamento na cooperação com a China', 15 November

Kiala, C. (2010) 'China–Angola aid relations: strategic cooperation for development?', *South African Journal of International Affairs*,17(1): 6–9

Kurtenbach, E. (2007) 'Chinese builder defends Angola deal', *Business Day*, 27 March, http://www.businessday.co.za/articles/topstories.aspx?ID=BD4A422017, accessed 2 April 2007

Levkowitz, L., Ross, M.M. and Warner, J.R. (2009) 'The 88 Queensway Group: a case study in Chinese investors' operations in Angola and beyond', Washington, US–China Economic and Security Review Commission, http://www.uscc.gov/The_88_Queensway_Group.pdf, accessed 12 April 2012

Macauhub (2009) 'Government approves credit line provided by Portugal', 12 June

Marques de Morais, R. (2010a) 'Angola's MPs and business dealings', *Pambazuka News* 464, 6 January, http://www.pambazuka.org/en/category/features/61246, accessed 12 April 2012

Marques de Morais, R. (2010b) 'The self-dealings of Sonangol's CEO ', *Pambazuka News*, 487, 24 June, http://www.pambazuka.org/en/category/features/65422, accessed 12 April 2012

Marques de Morais, R. (2010c) 'The Angolan presidency: the epicentre of corruption', *Pambazuka News*, 493, 5 August, http://www.pambazuka.org/en/category/features/66476, accessed 12 April 2012

Marques de Morais, R. (2011) 'The new imperialism: China in Angola', *World Affairs Journal*, March/April: 67–74

Martins, V. (2010) 'Keeping business in and politics out: Angola's multi-vector foreign policy', Lisbon, Portuguese Institute of International Relations and Security

Messiant, C. (2007) 'The mutation of hegemonic domination', in Chabal, P. and Vidal, N. (eds) *Angola: The Weight of History*, London, Hurst Publishers

Migdal, J.S. (1988) *Strong Societies and Weak States*, Princeton, Princeton University Press

Novo Jornal (2010) 'Sonangol cria imobiliária com estatuto de subsidiária', 2 August

Orre, A. (2010) 'Who's to challenge the party-state in Angola? Political space and opposition in parties and civil society', paper presented at CMI and IESE conference 'Election processes, liberation movements and democratic change in Africa', Maputo, 8–11 April

Pawson, L. (2008) 'The Angolan elections: politics of no change', *Open Democracy*, 25 September

Pinto de Andrade, V. (2007) 'A China e a assistência ao desenvolvimento de Angola', unpubished paper, Luanda, Universidade Católica de Angola

Reno, W. (2000) 'The (real) war economy in Angola', in Cilliers, J. and Dietrich, C. (eds) *Angola's war economy: The Role of Oil and Diamonds*, Pretoria, Institute for Security Studies

Schmitz, H. (2007) 'Reducing complexity in the industrial policy debate', *Development Policy Review*, 25(4): 417–28

Shaxson, N. (2007) *Poisoned Wells: The Dirty Politics of African Oil*, New York, Palgrave Macmillan

Soares de Oliveira, R. (2007a) 'Business success, Angola-style: post-colonial politics and the rise and rise of Sonangol', *Journal of Modern African Studies*, 45(4): 595–619

Soares de Oliveira, R. (2007b) *Oil and Politics in the Gulf of Guinea*, London, Hurst Publishers

Sogge, D. (2009) 'Angola: "failed" yet "successful"', Working Paper 81, Fundación par alas Relaciones Internacionales y el Diálogo Exterior

Snow, P. (1988) *The Star Raft*, London, Weidenfeld and Nicolson

Staniland, M. (1985) *What is Political Economy? A Study of Social Theory and Underdevelopment*, New Haven, Yale University Press

Taylor, I. (2006) 'PRC relations with Angola', in Taylor, I. (ed) *China and Africa: Engagement and Compromise*, London, Routledge

van de Walle, N. (2001) *African Economies and the Politics of Permanent Crisis*, Cambridge, Cambridge University Press

Vines, A., Wong, L., Weimer, M. and Campos, I. (2009) *Thirst for African Oil: Asian National Oil Companies in Nigeria and Angola*, London, Chatham House

Vines, A., Wong, L., Weimer, M. and Campos, I. (2011) *Petrolíferas Nacionais Asiáticas na Nigéria e em Angola*, London, Chatham House

4

China and Angola: a strategic partnership?

Sofia Fernandes

China and the liberation movements in Angola

The involvement of China in Angola in the 20th century dates back to the beginning of the pro-independence struggle started in 1961.[1] At first China tried to support the Marxist-inspired Movimento Popular de Libertação de Angola (MPLA), but disagreements within the movement resulted in its express pro-Soviet alignment (Schneidman, 2007). Considering the anti-Soviet character of China's foreign policy in the African continent, Chinese leaders leaned toward support for the Frente Nacional de Libertação de Angola (FNLA) and also the União Nacional para a Independência Total de Angola (UNITA), both recognised as legitimate liberation movements in Angola by the Organisation of African Unity (OAU). The strategic position of the People's Republic of China within the region was also more favourable to the FNLA and UNITA movements, both positioned next to Zaire's frontiers (north and north-east for FNLA, central and central-east for UNITA). China had military bases in Zaire, accessible to both FNLA and UNITA but not to MPLA, whose constituency was based along the coastline, mainly in the area surrounding Luanda and eastwards to Malange and with an important group of supporters in the south in the neighbouring area of Benguela, Angola's second largest city (Pélissier and Wheeler 2009).

The contours of China's involvement with FNLA and UNITA are not uncontroversial but what can be acknowledged from the relevant literature is that China had suggested providing support

68

to both movements. In 1963 the Chinese minister of foreign affairs, Chen Yi, met with the leader of FNLA, Holden Roberto, in Nairobi, and the leader of UNITA, Jonas Savimbi, was invited for a visit to Beijing in 1964. According to Taylor (2006) and to other accounts, FNLA received most of its weaponry from China and the movement relied almost exclusively on Zairean and Chinese military support from 1960 to 1974 (Monteiro 2001). UNITA's leader, Jonas Savimbi, along with other political cadres of the movement, was given military training and Maoist indoctrination in China, a fact that came to be decisive to the organising structure and ideological principles present in the early days of the movement (Chiwale 2008) and also in the relations that China later forged with MPLA.

In the late 1960s, according to Taylor (2006), UNITA was the main liberation movement receiving support from Beijing. Beijing was aware that FNLA was losing the battle: the movement did not have any specific ideology, it was very personalised and leader centred and accepted support regardless of its sources and conditions. Moreover FNLA was a heavily ethnic-based group, with its constituency among the Bakongo[2]. It was initially named the União das Populações do Norte de Angola (UPNA) and later the União das Populações de Angola (UPA) before finally becoming FNLA.

In 1971, as the Cultural Revolution came to an end, anti-Soviet sentiment reached its peak and China tried a new approach towards MPLA, inviting its leader, Agostinho Neto, for a visit to Beijing. In the aftermath of the visit the verdict of the Chinese authorities was that the MPLA leader was too 'pro-Russian' (Schneidman 2007) and the Chinese preferred to keep providing support to the other contending nationalist movements (mainly to UNITA) that were considered more viable and more likely to come to power in the future. In 1975, when MPLA declared the independence of Angola, China refused to recognise the newly independent country. Relations between the two countries were severely damaged by China's support for FNLA, which was accused of the massacres that took place at the beginning of the war for independence. These targeted not only the white Portuguese owners of coffee plantations in the area of Dembos in the province of Bengo (north-west of Luanda) but also their

Angolan employees, usually coming from Huambo in the Central Highlands of Angola, an area that later came to be dominated by UNITA and its Ovimbundu-based constituency. China's support to UNITA was thought to be maintained for some time after and throughout the 1990s, as weapons of light artillery as well as anti-personnel mines were found in northern Angola (Campos and Vines 2008).

Despite the fact that formal diplomatic relations were established in 1983, eight years after independence, the first real event in Chinese–Angolan relations was in 1999 when the first meeting was held of the Sino-Angolan Joint Economic and Trade Commission (Campos and Vines 2008). In the 1980s defence cooperation was dominant in the relations between the two countries, particularly given the civil war, but it acquired an economic emphasis when the internal conflict came to an end in 2002. The inclination for the immediate intervention of China's government officers and state banks in Angola following the death of Jonas Savimbi in 2002, derives to a large extent from the post-independence defence deals with the MPLA regime and also from Angola's express support of the Beijing regime following the Tiananmen massacre (Taylor 2009: 14), an attitude shared by many other African regimes.

The reorientation of China's foreign policy

In line with China's relations with Angola briefly synthesised above, a reorientation of China's policy vis-à-vis the third world took place in the aftermath of the Tiananmen incidents, considering the sanctions imposed by Western countries. In fact, according to Zhang (2004), the first leader to visit China after Tiananmen was the president of Burkina Faso, following a set of declarations from several African leaders in support of the Chinese government stating that the events were a matter of Chinese internal affairs. Also, at the end of the cold war Chinese leaders took their time in reacting to the fall of the Soviet Union and in stating their position regarding the new world order. Zhao (2004: 141) argues that the Chinese leadership 'normatively' wanted a multipolar world order, but that de facto the leadership acknowledged a unipolar world order. A speech given by Liu Yushan (a

Communist Party of China Politburo member) in 2009 stated that 'among China's great accomplishments since 1949 is the fact that it has substantially enhanced its comprehensive national power' and has 'noticeably upgraded its international position' (*People's Daily* 2009).

An essential feature of the reorientation of China's foreign policy towards Africa during the 1990s is the quest for natural resources, predominantly oil. In 2009, five years earlier than expected, China overtook the United States in primary energy consumption (*Wall Street Journal* 2010).[3] China pursued a strategy of establishing various energy-supply contracts, particularly those concerned with oil, given the need to satisfy China's increasing demand for energy that derived mainly from its development model, itself heavily based on energy-intensive industries. In view of the need to formalise the increasing strategic importance of Africa to China, it published its Africa Policy Paper in 2006 outlining its core aims and objectives in seeking cooperation with African 'partners'.

Besides oil, the construction sector has been one area where China has acquired prominence in Africa. This is true also for Angola, considering that according to Corkin (2011) the accumulated value of construction contracts in the hands of Chinese companies has surpassed $22 million in 2009. According to the Portuguese International Trade and Investment Agency (AICEP) (2010), in 2008 China became the main client of Angola, absorbing 35.4 per cent of its exports, ranking as the country's second supplier and accounting for 16 per cent of its total imports. It is important to recognise here that according to calculations based on data collected from the Agência Nacional para o Investimento Privado (ANIP – the Angolan National Private Investment Agency), 77.3 per cent of overall recorded Chinese private investment from 1990 to November 2010, a total amount of $338 million, was in the construction sector.

The bulk of Chinese private investment in Angola was made from 2008 onwards. According to calculations from data extracted from the Trade Law Centre for Southern Africa (TRALAC 2010), Chinese imports from Angola declined from $22 billion in 2008 to $14 billion in 2009, constituting a 37 per cent decrease and signalling a sharp fall in the value of Angolan crude oil sales to China.[4]

This fact seems to be attributable mostly to the abrupt decrease from a peak in oil prices in 2008 (above $100 a barrel) and not to a decrease in volume of Chinese oil imports from Angola.

The energy issue

Two important points to note in understanding the importance of energy issues in China–Angola cooperation are that Angola has increased its oil production exponentially since 2000 – from 736,000 barrels per day (bpd) to 1.7 million bpd in 2010 (OPEC 2010: 28) – and that in January 2007 it joined the Organisation of the Petroleum Producing Countries (OPEC), which obliges the country to comply with quota productions.

In 2008 Angola became the most important oil supplier to China. The oil sale agreements with China are not simple 'export the product and receive the payment' deals. They have been negotiated with the Chinese government in exchange for generous and renewed credit lines. In fact the regular debt service of the loans is made from an account where the Angolan government receives the payments accruing from the sale to China of 10,000 bpd in the first two years of the loan repayment, changing to 15,000 bpd afterwards (AFRODAD 2006) at a pre-negotiated contract price. Moreover, the oil sold to China to service the debt of these oil-backed loans represented only a small fraction – 1.5 to 2.5 per cent – of the total oil output of 596,000 barrels sold to China that same year (Alves 2010). The idea that China has been buying the larger part of Angolan oil at on-the-spot market prices, according to daily market Brent oil prices, was corroborated in an interview with a former employee of Total Fina Angola[5] which acknowledges that the majority of Sonangol oil sales are made at 'offload prices'.

Besides the supply of oil linked to loans, China has also been looking for joint ventures in the exploration of oil blocks in Angola. The assignment of 50 per cent of the profitable block 18 to Sonangol Sinopec International (SSI) in 2004, a company that originated in the joint venture between Sonangol and Sinopec, has astonished ONGC Videsh, the Indian national oil company, to whom Shell, in charge of the block's exploration, had agreed to sell 50 per cent of its equity (Vines et al 2009). The prospects of Chinese firms in the subsequent licensing bid, in 2007, were damaged by the disagreement between Sonangol and Sinopec negotiators concerning the target market for the product of the proposed Lobito refinery. The project for the construction of the refinery in the city of Lobito on the south-western coast of Angola is one cherished by the Angolan authorities – it would enable the country to increase its self-sufficiency in the downstream oil industry. According to the press (Macauhub 2007), Sonangol CEO Manuel Vicente stated that China was trying to divert all the production to China. In contrast, Sonangol's objective was to produce for its internal market, as well as for regional and Western markets (Alves 2010), which would turn Angola into a self-sufficient oil producer and exporter, with enhanced comprehensive power coming from its acreage in the oil industry. These disagreements meant that the refinery project did not materialise as Sinopec, the Chinese counterpart, withdrew. As a result, China was punished and its aspirations in the Angolan oil industry were put on hold in the 2007 oil bid. Sinopec originally made a joint bid with the other 'dragon-head'[6] national oil company, China National Offshore Oil Corporation (CNOOC), for a 20 per cent stake in bloc 32 operated by Total, being relinquished by North-American Marathon, but in a similar fashion to what happened in bloc 18, Sonangol decided to make use of its pre-emptive rights and intervened in the deal, this time against the Sinopec/CNOOC consortium, apparently based on commercial considerations (*Wall Street Journal* 2009), thereby issuing a clear message concerning Sinopec's behaviour in the Lobito refinery project.

The national reconstruction goal

The construction sector has become increasingly important as a result of China's engagement in the country. China is often praised as a vital partner in the reconstruction of Angola given that all other traditional donors and partners turned down the request of the Angolan government for an international donors' conference in 2002, after the death of the main opposition leader, Jonas Savimbi, finally put an end to the civil war. The refusal of the international donor community was based on concerns about the lack of transparency in Angolan national accounts. In the reconstruction context, it is worth mentioning the declining attention given by OECD official development aid to economic infrastructure in the last two decades – the priority has been given instead to good governance, technical assistance and social infrastructure such as schools and health centres (Oya 2011). Pezzini (2011) adds that traditional donors have assigned 65 per cent of aid to the social sector and only 17 per cent to infrastructure; whereas China by the end of 2000 had assigned 61 per cent of its concessional loans to economic infrastructure and 4.1 per cent to agriculture, inspired by the Chinese saying, 'to end poverty, build a road'.

For Angola this approach was particularly important considering that the country was helplessly in need of infrastructure after more than 40 years of continued armed conflict. The transparency condition imposed by the IMF was not welcomed by the political class, who argued that work needed to be done at a fast pace given the poor living conditions throughout the country and that issues of accessibility by land were a significant problem.[7] Up to 2002 the inhabitants of Luanda were trapped within a security perimeter of approximately 50km around the city, limited by the cities of Cacuaco and Viana and the Kwanza River. Beyond this it was impossible to go anywhere since roads were terribly damaged (and often populated by landmines), which added to the possibility of being caught in a UNITA raid. As an example of the bad road conditions a road trip to Uíge (400km) could take up to 8 days, and to Saurimo (around 600km), in the northeastern province of Lunda Sul, up to 10 days.

So as soon as the war really came to an end in 2002, the reconstruction of the country's shattered infrastructure had to start immediately, since most of the deprivations were blamed on the war effort. At this point China came along as the 'perfect' financing partner. Chinese construction companies were willing to work in extremely hard conditions[8] that for a Western or even Korean company would mean raising their costs hugely, adding to the difficulty in recruiting personnel. Low and Jiang (2003) argue that Chinese construction companies had significant comparative advantages including the abundance of highly motivated, low-priced manpower with the ability to adapt to different environments, along with the low costs of machinery, materials and equipment imported from China.

Chinese construction companies in Angola are often accused of employing an insignificant percentage of Angolan workers, relying almost entirely on their own workforce (including low-skilled Chinese workers) who compete with the majority of the unemployed male Angolan workforce. According to the General Angolan Labour Law, 70 per cent of the workforce on a construction site must be Angolan, but that quota can be overcome if the contractor proves that they are not able to find a national worker with the necessary skills to perform a certain job (e.g. hydraulic engineer).[9] The problem of the scarcity of qualified human resources in Angola is very significant, owing partly to the disruptive effects of the long-lasting internal conflict but also to Angola's low population density of around 14.8 inhabitants per square kilometre,[10] most of which is highly concentrated in the capital city of Luanda.[11] Bearing this in mind there may be pressure on Chinese construction companies to take on Chinese expatriate workers in places less populated than Luanda, given that a very limited workforce – even in less-specialised construction tasks – is available locally. Therefore the recruitment of workers from China is posited as a necessary option for these companies. Adding to this is also the argument of 'efficiency' with several Chinese contractors arguing that they cannot comply with project deadlines if they recruit as many Angolans as legally defined – they argue that the national workers do not have the necessary skills and are not used to the Chinese pace of work.[12] Another account[13] suggests that the work model of Chinese companies has astonished both the population and other companies competing in the construction market in Angola – Chinese workers live at their worksites, allowing them not to waste time with daily commutes to and from work, as well as to save money for their companies in accommodation costs, an issue that absorbs a considerable share of the maintenance costs of any company operating in Angola.[14] They are also said to work extra hours on an incentive-based pay system.

The projects contracted under the credit lines coming from China were reportedly subject to strict supervision by the ministry of finance in regard to the number of Angolan nationals recruited against Chinese workers and present at any time on a construction site and also the progress of the approved project. The work done by Chinese construction companies, in both the public and private sectors, is thought to have no significant difference in quality from the work performed by companies from other countries present in the market (be it South African, Portuguese or Korean), with insufficiencies being blamed on the government supervision of the work performed or on the government's approval of projects (since if the project itself is not good the work will never be distinguished for its superior quality). Another characteristic of Chinese construction companies that is often noted is the pace of their workers and their ability to meet and go beyond specified objectives, as the Chinese are said to define very clear milestones for the daily assessment of work on a construction site. According to one account: 'They (the Chinese) have an approach that is more conceptualised ... they see the whole picture quicker ... they see it in a long term perspective and have something that we don't have, they have milestones'.[15]

The claim that Chinese companies recruit their workers mainly from China and that this workforce is predominantly made up of non-skilled labour seems to be in contradiction with some of the data that I collected during my fieldwork – Chinese construction companies in Angola are seen as having adapted to market needs and as having professionals in all sorts of specialised functions. That finding is also corroborated in the literature concerning the internationalisation of Chinese construction companies (Low and Jiang 2004: 724) acknowledge a five- to six-fold rise in the operating costs of Chinese companies undertaking projects abroad from the beginning of the 1990s to the year 2000, owing partially to the need to recruit more specialised workers (e.g. engineers, architects) and also to some reluctance on the side of Chinese workers to work under tough conditions in developing countries. According to the authors, although the recruiting of workers in less specialised functions started being done locally on the grounds of cost, the recruitment of Chinese engineers is seen as still less onerous to the company than employing non-Chinese engineers.

However, the large influxes of Chinese workers into the Angolan economy, where the unemployment rate is 28 per cent[16] (African Economic Outlook 2011), is causing distress and anxiety in society. While some people emphasise the benefits to Angola's economy of the influx of Chinese manpower in the first phase of reconstruction (from 2004 up to 2008) others signal the adverse effects of Chinese companies' recruitment strategies. On top of this lies the opacity regarding Chinese residents in the country. According to an interview (Angonoticias 2011) given by the Chinese ambassador in Angola, Zhang Bolun, in March 2011 the number of Chinese residents in the country varies between 60,000 and 70,000 but the secrecy surrounding the figures (which are not disclosed by the Angolan immigration services) makes room for imagination and speculation. Some accounts even situate the number at around 400,000 workers.[17] Some of these workers apparently manage to stay in the country and start their own private businesses (the numbers are not available but the empirical evidence is). The Chinese are today a permanent feature in Angola, not only as workers of big state-owned construction enterprises, but also in the private construction sector. Advertisements for Chinese-owned construction firms offering their services can be found in the daily newspapers. In fact, the Chinese are competing heavily in the private housing sector, as evidence was found that they are carrying on the construction of private houses aimed at different income levels – be it in the poorer outskirts of Luanda or in the fashionable residential area of Talatona. Private residential condominiums are also being built by Chinese companies such as Jardim do Éden in the district of Kilamba Kiaxi.[18]

The distribution sector

Besides oil and construction, the Chinese are also actively engaged in both the retail and wholesale trades. The creation of the Forum for Economic and Trade Cooperation between China and Portuguese-speaking Countries in 2003, was a clear sign of Chinese companies' interest in the Angolan market. According to an interview with an official close to the Angolan Chamber of Trade and Industry, this forum has been hosting an increasing number of Chinese companies, 'with the goal to sell their finished product in Angola, but not to invest or make joint-ventures'.[19]

The Angolan Law of Private Investment (ANIP 2004) defines as 'foreign investment' any investment where the capital originates outside Angola, regardless of the nationality of the investor, i.e. both nationals and foreign residents in the country can be considered to be foreign investors. To qualify for benefits and fiscal exemptions there are requirements such as a minimum amount invested of $100,000[20] – or $150,000 in the case of a joint venture with an Angolan partner. These exemptions are important as they include fiscal exemptions on imports of machinery and equipment, or of intermediate products, exemption of up to 15 years on corporate tax benefits (*Imposto Industrial sobre Benefícios*) and also tax deductions on the expenses incurred in the construction of infrastructure (ICEX 2011).

To initiate the process with ANIP it is highly advisable that the amount to be invested is already transferred to this state department. As this comes as an administrative request it can either be approved or not approved. However if the investor has capital sourced in Angola and does not intend to repatriate benefits (i.e. is Angolan) he or she will not have to comply with this legislation and is only required to make investments of $1,000 for limited liability companies (LLCs) and $20,000 for public limited companies (PLCs). So in the relevant guidance it is suggested that a foreign investor may get an Angolan partner to start the investment registration procedures with ANIP. The legal procedures mentioned are useful for understanding the difficulties and restrictions on starting a business in Angola, as well as for understanding the obstacles encountered in tracking Chinese owners in retail trading in Angola. In order to circumvent restrictions on retail trade licensing, Chinese traders, according to some accounts, have been concentrating efforts on wholesale trade, supplying many of the capital's street vendors, called *zungueiros*, from their warehouses in the district of São Paulo in Luanda. At this point it is important to emphasise the importance of the informal sector to the economic structure of the country, which is most significant in the city of Luanda. According to the UNDP (2000), 41 per cent of the population in Luanda aged between 15 and 60 years was employed in the informal sector. A National Statistics Institute household survey conducted in 2000 (INE 2000) showed that on average 62.8 per cent of the working population identified an informal sector-related activity as their main means of subsistence.

According to an interview with a government officer[21] the predominance of informal trade in Luanda is due to a great extent to the restrictions involved in the licensing of any commercial activity and those concerning the share capital of any new company. The need for an Angolan business partner to hold 50 per cent of the share capital of the company discourages foreigners, including the Chinese, from engaging in formal retail trade activities, namely in the selling of garments, shoes and light consumer goods. As for the wholesale trade, the authorities apparently facilitate the activities of Chinese businessmen. The low prices of products coming from China are attractive to street vendors, allowing them to obtain additional profits from their sales. This is an important social issue as street vendors, who make up a considerable part of the trade in the informal sector, constitute the lower strata of the pyramid of agents operating in Luanda's informal sector, according to Lopes (2006). Further, Chinese middlemen are also very important in cross-border trade, working as intermediaries for Angolan traders in their trips to China, with the purpose of acquiring all sorts of products to sell in the informal market though their personal network of relations.

Concluding remarks

The relations between China and Angola have been acquiring significance since 2002, after the country finally entered an internal peace period. The presentation of China as a strategic partner – with both the financial resources, as well as its companies and personnel (i.e. with both the financial resources and the tools) – has been praised by the political elite in Angola. China is generally described as a strategic ally, to whom Angola owes its first steps towards rehabilitation. However, the official discourse concerning the importance of China as a strategic partner to Angola has been shifting. Originally, at the beginning of the reconstruction process (i.e. from 2004, when the first Chinese-financed infrastructural projects started, up to the 2008 legislative elections) the role of the Chinese model of cooperation and assistance was praised. However, from 2008 onwards there seems to be an emerging concern linked to the growing engagement of Chinese companies in the economy of Angola, and specifically to do with Chinese manpower in the country's economy.

On the side of China, the overall assessment of the Sino-Angolan partnership seems to be seen in very positive terms: the country has been the primary recipient of Angolan oil since 2008 and China has also been acquiring significance in the construction industry. Chinese construction companies, mostly state owned or owned by local governments, are actively engaged in the construction or rehabilitation of the main economic infrastructures of the country. Chinese companies have also been charged with the rehabilitation of the main highways, such as the roads linking Luanda to Benguela and Luanda to Malange as well as both the Benguela railway (which in the colonial era carried the majority of exports of mineral resources from Democratic Republic of Congo and Zambia) and the railway linking Luanda to Malange (a line that serves also Luanda's metropolitan area). The fact that there is a widespread engagement of the Chinese community in a variety of sectors of the country's economy – as wholesale traders, in the private construction business, as growers and vendors of fruit and vegetables, as urban/rural traders – are signs that Chinese workers entering the country have been moving away from having the status of controlled contract workers on limited-duration projects and are now beginning to settle in the country.

From an Angolan perspective, this partnership allowed the introduction of a new, more competitive impulse at both the political and business levels. At the political level the partnership with China allowed the diversification of financial partners and enabled the government to avoid IMF conditionalities and the focus on measures needed to meet the Millennium Development Goals. For Angola these demands were specifically around the transparency of public accounts and the need for good governance, as well as the repayment of debt to Paris Club creditors. The IMF was not willing to provide new loans to the country since Angola stopped paying its debt in 1986. The organisation of a donors' conference was not considered suitable given the previous episodes of default on debt repayments, added to the fact that it is an oil-producing country, considered capable of generating its own substantial national revenues. By the time the principal in debt was reimbursed to Paris Club creditors in 2006 (an amount of $2.6 billion) Chinese companies had already done two years of work in the country (INE 2000).

The entrance of Chinese companies into the oil sector can, however, be considered not as successful as might have been expected from the perspective of the Chinese authorities: the bids of Chinese companies in oil auctions are totally interlocked with the political agenda of the Angolan government, and the 'know-how' to negotiate in the Angolan political arena still seems in relatively short supply on the part of Chinese diplomats and high-level political officers. The construction sector seems to be where the Chinese are gaining a more substantial foothold and recognition in Angola, despite the fact that the recruitment policies of Chinese companies are a cause for concern regarding the degree of local people's involvement in the reconstruction process. In the distribution sector it is important to mention the role of Chinese traders not only in wholesale trade but also as middlemen between urban and rural areas.[22]

The recent involvement of the Chinese in Angola has developed in the context of a major economic boom in Angola accruing from high oil prices and the end of the war. Considering their long term approach with its origins in Asian Confucian values, as well as their continuing and widespread engagement with the fabric of Angola's economy, it is expected that their presence in the country is an enduring and not just a seasonal feature.

Notes

1. Historians find it difficult to date the onset of the national liberation war against the Portuguese: some accounts tell us that the armed conflict began on 4 February 1961 with the assault on St Paul prison in Luanda (claimed by MPLA militants); other accounts date the beginning of the armed conflict to 15 March in the same year, when the União das Populações de Angola (UPA), later renamed to Frente Nacional de Libertação de Angola (FNLA), started the massacres in the northern coffee-producing farms.
2. An ethnic group that extends also to Congo and which previously formed the ancient kingdom of Congo. See Pélissier and Wheeler (2009).
3. Statistics from the *Wall Street Journal* (2010) are based on statistics on energy consumption from the International Energy Agency 2010, http://online.wsj.com/article/SB10001424052748703720504575376712353150310.html, accessed 27 May 2011
4. Crude oil makes up for more than 99 per cent of Angolan exports to China since 1995.
5. Interview with an ex-cadre of Total Fina Angola, 3 February 2011.
6. Dragon-head companies are state-renovated companies, which because of their size and strategic importance were designated by the government

as companies to internationalise, receiving express administrative and financial state incentives.

7. Interview with a member of the Angolan ministry of finance, 2 February 2011, Luanda.
8. Interview with the manager of a company responsible for supervision and consultation in the construction sector in Angola, Luanda, 3 February 2011.
9. Interview with a member of the Angolan ministry of finance, 2 February 2011, Luanda Law nr 2/2000, 11 February 2000.
10. With an estimated population of 18.5 million inhabitants in 2009 (World Bank statistics) and a territory of 1,246,700km^2, its population density is around 14.8 inhabitants per square kilometre.
11. Luanda's population is estimated at 4 million people.
12. Interview with a member of the Angolan ministry of finance, Luanda, 4 February 2011.
13. Interview with a construction company manager, Luanda, 3 February 2011.
14. Luanda was considered the most expensive city for expatriate managers in 2010 by the 'Cost of living survey' by Mercer Consultant (*Público* 2010), http://economia.publico.pt/Noticia/luanda-e-a-cidade-mais-cara-do-mundo_1444346, accessed 29 March 2011
15. Interview with a member of the Angolan ministry of finance, Luanda, 2 February 2011.
16. Taking into account the huge differences across the country, the unemployment rate in the city of Luanda is 17 per cent.
17. Interview with an Angolan entrepreneur in the telecommunications sector, Lisbon, 18 January 2011.
18. Interviews with different actors.
19. Interview with a member of the Angolan Chamber of Trade and Industry, Luanda, 10 February 2011.
20. ICEX (2011) suggests that ANIP was not approving projects under $250,000.
21. Interview with a member of the treasury department, ministry of finance, Luanda, 9 February 2011.
22. According to an interview with an academic, Luanda, 7 February 2010, in the colonial period it was the Portuguese 'bush trader' who took light manufactured products such as salt, matches, fish, textiles and 'panos' to rural inland inhabitants and brought back with him to the city, rice, corn and cassava. Apparently some Chinese traders are already engaged in this rural/urban trade.

References

African Economic Outlook (2011) 'Africa and its emergent partners', African Development Bank, http://www.africaneconomicoutlook.org/po/countries/southern-africa/angola, accessed 27 May 2011

AFRODAD (African Forum and Network on Debt and Development) (2006)

'A critical assessment of Chinese development assistance in Africa, Angola', http://www.afrodad.org/downloads/publications/Angola%20 Factsheet.pdf, accessed 2 March 2012

AICEP Portugal Global (2010) 'Ficha de mercado-Angola', Portuguese International Trade and Investment Agency (July)

Alves, A. (2010) 'The oil factor in Sino-Angolan relations at the start of the 21st century', *SAIIA Occasional Paper*, 55

Angonotícias (2011) 'China já emprestou USD 15 mil milhões a Angola', 9 March, http://www.angonoticias.com/full_headlines.php?id=30845, accessed 9 June 2011

ANIP (2004) 'Colectânea de legislação, lei de bases do investimento privado', lei nº 11/03 de 13 de Maio

Campos, I. and Vines, A. (2008) 'Angola and China: a pragmatic partnership', working paper presented at a CSIS conference 'Prospects for improving US–China–Africa relations', http://www.chathamhouse.org/sites/default/ files/public/Research/Africa/angolachina_csis.pdf, accessed 17 April 2012

Chiwale, S. (2008) *Cruzei-me com a história*, Lisboa, Sextante Editora

CIA World Factbook (2011) 'Angola', https://www.cia.gov/library/ publications/the-world-factbook/geos/ao.html, accessed 26 May 2011

Corkin, L. (2011) 'Uncovering agency: Angola's management of relations with China', paper presented at the conference 'China and Angola: challenges and opportunities', Luanda, 31 January

ICEX (2011) 'Guía de la inversión en Angola', prepared by the economic and trade section of the Spanish embassy in Luanda, February

INE (2000) 'Inquérito às Despesas e Receitas dos Agregados Familiares', Luanda

Lopes, C. M. (2006) 'Candongueiros, kinguilas, roboteiros e zungueiros: uma digressão pela economia informal de Luanda', *Lusotopie*, 13(1): 163–83

Low, S. P. and Jiang, H. (2003) 'Internationalization of Chinese construction enterprises', *Journal of Construction Engineering and Management*, 129(6): 589–98

Low, S.P. and Jiang, H.B. (2004) 'A comparative study of top British and Chinese international contractors in the global market', *Construction Management and Economics*, 22: 717–31

Macauhub (2007) 'Pequim desvaloriza fim da parceria entre Sonangol e Sinopec', 9 March, http://www.macauhub.com.mo/pt/2007/03/09/2655/ accessed 27 May 2011

Monteiro, F. (2001) 'Ver para crer', *O Mundo em Português*, 22–23, Instituto de Estudos Estratégicos e Internacionais, http://www.ieei.pt/publicacoes/ artigo.php?artigo, accessed 28 May 2011

OPEC (2010) Annual Statistical Bulletin, Organization of the Petroleum Exporting Countries, Vienna

Oya, C. (2011) Seminar 'China como fonte de financiamento para África: hipóteses, mitos e realidades no desenvolvimento africano', ISEG, Lisbon, 6 May

Pélissier, R. and Wheeler, D. (2009) *História de Angola*, Lisboa, Tinta da China

People's Daily (2009) 'Stimulate a passion for patriotism, inspire national spirit and pool the people's efforts', 14 July, cit. in Kaufman, A. (2010) 'The "century of humiliation", then and now: Chinese perceptions of the international order', *Pacific Focus*, 25(1): 1–33

Pezzini, M. (2011) Address of the Director of the OECD Development Centre at the launch of 'African economic outlook' 2011, in Lisbon, 6 June

Público (2010) 'Luanda é a cidade mais cara do mundo', 29 June, http:// economia.publico.pt /Noticia/luanda-e-a-cidade-mais-cara-do-mundo_1444346, accessed 26 May 2011

Schneidman, W. (2007) *Confronto em África – Washington e a Queda do Império Colonial Português*, Lisboa, Edições Tribuna

Taylor, I. (2006) 'PRC relations with Angola', in Taylor, Ian (ed) *China and Africa: Engagement and Compromise*, London, Routledge

Taylor, I. (2009) *China's New Role in Africa*, London, Lynne Rienner Publishers

TRALAC (Trade Law Centre for Southern Africa) (2010) 'Africa's trading relationship with China 2010', www.tralac.org, accessed 10 June 2011

UNDP (2000) *Poverty Alleviation Policy in Angola: Pursuing Equity and Efficiency*, Luanda

Vines, A., Wong, L., Weimer, M. and Campos, I. (2009) *Thirst for African Oil: Asian National Oil Companies in Nigeria and Angola*, London, Chatham House

Wall Street Journal (2009) 'Sonangol wants to block Marathon's stake sale to China', 12 September, http://www.marketwatch.com/story/sonangol-wants-to-block-marathons-stake-sale-to-china-2009-09-12, accessed 27 May 2011

Wall Street Journal (2010) 'China tops US in energy use', 18 July, http://online.wsj.com/article, accessed 27 May 2011

Zhang, H. (2004) 'A política chinesa em África', in Belluci, B. (ed) *Abrindo os Olhos para a China*, Rio de Janeiro, Universidade Cândido Mendes

Zhao, S. (2004) 'Beijing's perception after the Tiananmen incident' in Zhao, S. (ed) *Chinese Foreign Policy: Pragmatism and Strategic Behavior*, New York, ME Sharpe

5

China's Angolan oil deals 2003–11

Markus Weimer and Alex Vines

Over the last decade Angola has become increasingly important as a source of oil for China. This chapter assesses how China has accessed Angolan oil and how it has secured this through infrastructure deals. It is an update on the basis of the Angola section in *Thirst for African Oil* which was published by Chatham House in August 2009.[1]

The Angolan context and the success of China

After the end of its civil war in 2002, Angola posted the highest increase in oil output (ahead of Russia, Azerbaijan, Brazil, Libya and Kazakhstan). From 2004–05 Chinese oil companies began to secure oil blocks in Angola. Angola is today a key player in Africa's oil industry as a major producer and exporter, and in 2008 Angola briefly surpassed Nigeria as the leading sub-Saharan oil producer. In 2010 China's imports of crude from Angola stood at 18 per cent of the total (the same as Saudi Arabia), and for the period from January to June 2011, Angola was China's second most important supplier of crude oil (after Saudi Arabia and ahead of Iran).[2] In 2010, 45 per cent of total Angolan oil exports were to China, while the US was the destination of 23 per cent of Angolan oil.[3]

The success of the relationship between Angola and China is marked by two important features. The first is the success of Chinese oil strategies in Angola through the interlinking of state-directed businesses and diplomacy. Business vehicles established by Hong Kong-based private interests in partnership with the China Petroleum & Chemical Corporation (Sinopec), and the

Angolan national oil company (Sonangol) have served the Chinese well in building up a portfolio of joint ventures with the Angolan leadership that have extended beyond oil to construction, aviation and real estate across the world. The second is that, in contrast to the reluctance of Western donors to finance Angola's essential post-war reconstruction, China was quick to provide oil-backed loans for infrastructure.

Oil and reconstruction after the war: the contribution of China

MUTUAL BENEFIT

After the war ended, rapid reconstruction became the Angolan government's top priority. China, which established diplomatic relations with Angola in 1983, has played a particularly important role in assisting these efforts. Chinese financial and technical assistance has engaged in over 100 projects since 2004 in a number of areas, including energy, water, health, education, telecommunications, fisheries and public works. On the occasion of Chinese Prime Minister Wen Jibao's visit to Angola in June 2006, President dos Santos described bilateral relations as being 'mutually advantageous', and the partnership as being 'pragmatic', with no 'political preconditions'.[4]

By 2009, China had facilitated loans to Angola amounting to at least $13.4 billion (or, according to some estimates, up to $19.7 billion). In 2009–10 a further $10 billion worth of credit lines were signed.[5] President José Eduardo dos Santos visited Beijing twice in 2008, underlining the importance of this relationship for Angola. In return, China's Sinopec group initially obtained oil equity through the Sonangol Sinopec International (SSI) business vehicle in a valuable deep-water block, and later obtained equity stakes in three further offshore blocks and in pre-salt blocks (see below). President dos Santos touched the core of this in November 2007 when he stated that 'China needs natural resources and Angola wants development'.[6]

The visit of the vice president, and likely future secretary general of the Chinese communist party, Xi Jinping to Luanda in January 2011 further cemented the relationship. During Xi's visit new agreements were signed in the transportation, mining and construction sectors and an extension of credit lines was agreed. Xi noted that Chinese loans had 'reached $10 billion'.[7]

'Angola mode': oil-backed loans for infrastructure

Having become a net oil importer in 1993, China's demand for oil is growing exponentially. As a result of this increasing demand, since 2003 Chinese national oil companies (NOCs) have tried rapidly to acquire stakes in exploration and production projects in Angola, as well as purchasing more Angolan oil on the spot market. In early 2004, Sonangol opened its Sonasia office in Singapore, aimed at promoting the trade of Angolan crude oil to Asia.

The China Construction Bank (CCB) and Exim Bank provided the first funding for Angolan infrastructure development in 2002. The Angolan ministry of finance had little input into these arrangements since funding was provided directly to Chinese firms. Financial relations between China and Angola grew further in November 2003 when a framework agreement for new cooperation was formally signed by the two governments. On 21 March 2004, the first $2 billion financing package for public investment projects was approved. Since 2004 Angola has agreed to at least two oil-backed loans for Chinese financial assistance for key public investment projects in infrastructure, telecommunications and agro-businesses under the national reconstruction programme. China's Exim Bank is increasingly making use of this deal structure – known by the World Bank as the 'Angola mode' or 'resources for infrastructure' – whereby repayment of the loan for infrastructure development is made in natural resources.[8]

There are questions however regarding the quality of the infrastructure delivered in return for oil as well as the timelines involved. There were some stoppages in Chinese construction projects in late 2007 and in 2008 linked to the China International Fund (CIF, see below). For example, the Benguela railway line project was subject to a series of contractual revisions that followed the discovery by the Angolan authorities of 'irregularities' by Chinese firms. As a result the Angolan government decided to let the Chinese companies continue to lay the railway, but to invite other competitors to tender for complementary projects.[9]

The assistant director of the Benguela Railway Company confirmed that sixteen Chinese camps had been dismantled and revealed that the contract had been cancelled.[10] However, work on the railway restarted in October 2010. The project has grossed $1.8 billion to date and reconstruction is set to be completed towards the end of 2012, by which time an estimated four million passengers and 20 million tons of goods per annum will be transported along the line. Ambitious plans also exist to extend the line to DRC, Zambia and Zimbabwe.[11]

Sinopec's first steps

Following the opening of China's first credit line to Angola in March 2004, Sinopec acquired its first stake in Angola's oil industry in July of the same year – 50 per cent of the BP-operated block 18. Sonangol Sinopec International (SSI) was created to explore the stake on the block.[12] It is a joint venture majority-owned by Sinopec (55 per cent stake) with Beiya (now Dayuan) International Development Ltd, and China Sonangol International Holding Ltd (CSIH) holding 31.5 per cent and 13.5 per cent of SSI respectively.[13]

SSI obtained a seven-year loan that is covered by a pre-completion guarantee from Sinopec during construction. Sonangol had prepared the way for this deal with a previous $3 billion corporate deal signed in September 2005, sold in the Hong Kong market under Hong Kong law through Calyon.[14] This was the largest pre-export finance facility to date and *Trade & Forfaiting Review* called it 2005's deal of the year. It came about because of contractual restrictions on Sonangol at the time against seeking new credit. The deal also marked a new structure, with funds provided directly to CSIH rather than a special purpose vehicle (SPV). CSIH was able to raise the funds on the back of the long-term off-take agreement with the crude trader China International United Petroleum & Chemicals (Unipec).[15]

This was the first Sonangol deal to involve a Chinese off-taker; it amounted to a $3 billion loan that was to be paid back over a seven-year period by the delivery of Angolan crude to Unipec (at a rate of 40,000 barrels per day for the first three years).[16] Once this loan was syndicated, CSIH participated in the SSI project-finance facility through its 31.5 per cent equity stake of Dayuan International Development. This arrangement suits Sinopec well, enabling it to benefit from major technology transfer from the

Western companies leading the operations (BP is the operator in block 18) while still being granted a large share of the oil from these licences.

Sinopec's growth in Angola

In March 2005, during Chinese Vice Premier Zeng Peiyang's visit to Angola, nine cooperation agreements were signed, mostly related to energy. Sonangol also entered a long-term uplift agreement to supply oil to Unipec, which *Africa Energy Intelligence* estimated could result in Sinopec (as the parent company) lifting up to 100,000 barrels per day.[17] Additionally, the two parties signed a memorandum of understanding to jointly study plans for the exploration of the shallow offshore blocks 3/05 and 3/05A – previously known as block 3/80 – (see above) which had been withdrawn from Total in late 2004.[18] Later that year, Sonangol agreed that CSIH would acquire the 25 per cent stake.[19] CSIH does not have any Sinopec participation but the CSIH stake was handed over to SSI (where Sinopec holds a 55 per cent interest) in 2007.

In April and May 2006 Sonangol announced the winners of exploration licences for seven shallow- and deep-water concessions that had been put out to tender in November 2005. SSI acquired three new Angolan offshore oil blocks. It offered $750 million for 20 per cent of ENI-operated block 15 after failing to win the operatorship. SSI also made a record $2.2 billion signature bonus payment ($1.1 billion for each block) for the relinquished offshore blocks 17/06 (27.5 per cent) and 18/06 (40 per cent). This signature bonus payment is a record for Angola and suggests that Sinopec felt it needed to pay over the odds to secure this acreage despite the ongoing Chinese loans to the Angolan government. From these Angolan acquisitions SSI hoped to add approximately one billion barrels of equity oil from production over the next five years. Sinopec believed that blocks 15/06, 17/06 and 18/06 have proven reserves of 1.5 billion, 1 billion and 700 million barrels of oil respectively.[20]

Since 2004, China has obtained equity partnerships in Angolan deep-water oil blocks through Sinopec's majority in SSI and in shallow-water blocks through CSIH, a joint venture between Sonangol and Hong Kong-based private business interests. SSI was awarded equity in deep-water block 18 in 2004 and CSIH was awarded equity in blocks 3/05 and 3/05A in 2005. This was, however, turned over to SSI by 2007. SSI was awarded further equity in blocks 15/06, 17/06 and 18/06 (with Agip-ENI, Total and Petrobas being the respective operatorship winners) in the May 2006 oil licensing awards (although this was subsequently handed over to CSIH to hold, before being eventually returned to SSI – see below).[21] In the most recent pre-salt round (2011), CSIH consolidated its foothold in Angola (see table 5.1).

Inter-Chinese rivalry

Increasingly it is impossible to speak of 'China' as a unified homogeneous actor in Angola. This becomes clear when analysing the increasing number of different interests and actors that exist in the oil relations between Angola and China.

Sinopec Corporation's director and chairman of the third session of its board of directors, Dr Su Shulin, visited Luanda in April 2008. This was followed by a delegation from Zhen Hua Oil (an affiliate of NORINCO), who arrived in Luanda in March 2008 to sign a memorandum of understanding with Sonangol.[22] Chinese NOCs seem to be competing abroad.

This became much clearer in the 'Marathon saga': on 17 July 2009, it was announced that Marathon International Petroleum Angola Block 32 Ltd, a subsidiary of Marathon Oil, had entered into a definitive agreement with China National Offshore Oil Corporation (CNOOC) and Sinopec. Both companies were said to purchase an undivided 20 per cent participating interest in the production-sharing contract and joint operating agreement in block 32 for $1.3 billion, effective from 1 January 2009. Marathon Oil would have

Table 5.1 Chinese acquisition of Angolan oil blocks

Block	Company	Year acquired	Share (%)	Partner
19	CSIH	2011	10	BP [Op]
20	CSIH	2011	10	Cobalt [Op]
36	CSIH	2011	20	Conoco-Phillips [Op]
38	CSIH	2011	15	Statoil [Op]

retained a 10 per cent working interest. The companies expected to close the transaction by year-end 2009, subject to government and regulatory approvals.[23] Unusually, China National Petroleum Corporation (CNPC) also made a separate bid. As it turns out, CNOOC and Sinopec both lost out, as did CNPC. Sonangol decided to exercise its right of first refusal and offered the stake to CSIH.

Marathon, in one of their filings, stated the matter thus:

> During the first quarter 2010, we closed the sale of a 20 percent outside-operated interest in our E&P segment's Production Sharing Contract and Joint Operating Agreement in block 32 offshore Angola. We received net proceeds of $1.3 billion and recorded a pretax gain on the sale in the amount of $811 million. We retained a 10 per cent outside-operated interest in block 32.[24]

Manuel Vicente in his capacity as chief executive of Sonangol commented that, '[E]arlier this month Sonangol paid Marathon $1,000,300,000 (sic) for its 20 per cent share. We will add this share in block 32 to a joint venture we have with the Chinese called China Sonangol.'[25]

For the first time Chinese companies were openly competing among themselves for Angolan concessions and the biggest winner so far in this story was CSIH. Efforts also by CNOOC to partner up in 2011 with other Asian national oil companies like Indonesia's Pertamina for Angolan oil concessions have yet to show success.

Chinese opportunities in the financial crisis of 2008

Angolan officials admitted that falling oil prices in the wake of the international financial and economic crisis of 2008 have forced them to cut back on some of their $42 billion infrastructure plans for 2009. Not yet cash-strapped, but nevertheless concerned, President dos Santos visited China in December 2008 to seek guarantees that it would honour its Angolan loans and beef up its bilateral cooperation by extending new loans, and on 17 December 2008 Li Ruogu, the chairman and president of China Exim Bank, announced: 'We are planning to expand our cooperation with the Angolan ministry of finance.'[26]

Shortly after this pledge, China's commerce minister, Chen Deming, paid a two-day visit to Angola in January 2009, bringing with him a commitment from the China Development Bank to extend an additional loan to Angola worth at least $1 billion. This was confirmed by Chen Yuan, president of the China Development Bank, on 12 March 2009, following yet another meeting with President dos Santos.[27]

An initial agreement was signed in August 2008 and negotiations concerning the implementation of the agreement continued into 2009. This deal included construction of social housing, agriculture, transport and telecommunications. The former vice prime minister of Angola, and former head of the National Private Investment Agency (ANIP), Aguinaldo Jaime, confirmed in September 2008 that this loan would not be oil-backed.[28] He also told the Chinese media in January 2009 that President dos Santos had 'already received the president of the China–Africa Development Fund twice, clear proof of the degree to which Angola values its alliance with China.'[29] More loans from the Chinese Exim Bank are likely.

China's (then) ambassador to Angola, Zhang Bolun, met President dos Santos on 17 February 2009, after which he signalled that China was considering further financial assistance for infrastructure that would be 'properly implemented and protected from the world crisis'.[30] It is clear that since the legislative elections in 2008 the Angolan government has new priorities. Rapid post-conflict infrastructural development is less pressing, and delivering on some of MPLA's election promises such as diversification of the economy away from its dependence on oil and providing better services in health and education is higher up the agenda. The global economic downturn has also introduced cost-cutting and a focus on greater efficiency in government agencies – at least until oil prices recover and the end of the crisis. Ambassador Zhang Bolun was replaced by Gao Kexiang on 3 August 2011, and relations are unlikely to alter.

At the fourth session of the bilateral Angola–China Commission in March 2009, officials[31] committed themselves to increased financial cooperation by agreeing to put in place an investment guarantee scheme (emulating an earlier US agreement to the same effect). At the meeting China also offered a grant worth $34.15 million.

As mentioned above, the vice president of China, Xi Jinping, visited Luanda in January 2011, further cementing the relationship by signing a new set of agreements in the transportation, mining and construction sectors and another extension of credit lines was agreed. Xi's visit was followed by that of Wang Qishan, vice prime minister of China, in March 2011, Xu Baoecheng, the president of China Group, in October 2011, and a delegation headed by the deputy administrator of the Chinese State Administration for Science, Technology and Industry for National Defence (SASTIND), Wang Yi Ren, in November 2011. Wang Yi Ren met with the Angolan defence minister, Cândido Pereira Van-Dúnem, to explore military cooperation.

Chinese government officials believe that oil-backed loans are the most beneficial arrangement as they offer the greatest security and have regularly indicated this preference to their Angolan counterparts. The Angolans, however, seem to continue to want to move away from the 'Angola mode' approach. China is clearly seeking to secure more oil concessions but it is at the same time under pressure to provide better local content provisions in contracts for its companies.[32] Despite these differences, the bilateral relationship seems to be solid.

The China International Fund, GRN and local politics

From its genesis, oil-backed borrowing became an increasingly effective tool by which the Angolan presidency could secure spending priorities, bypassing the inefficiencies of the traditional financial system. It has become central to the exercise of power, and the Gabinete de Reconstrução Nacional (GRN) became its epicentre.

GRN was set up in 2005 to manage large investment projects and ensure rapid reconstruction of infrastructure prior to national elections. Initially headed by a military adviser to the president, General Hélder Vieira Dias 'Kopelipa', GRN was designed to provide work for the demobilised military in order to bring new dynamism to the reconstruction effort. Exclusively accountable to the Angolan presidency, it was also created on the assumption that the ministries would not have the capacity to manage the large inflows of money directed at the national reconstruction programme. GRN was designed to kick-start major prestige projects such as three railways, including the Caminhos de Ferro de Luanda railway project, drainage systems in Luanda, studies on a new city near Luanda, social housing, administration, and the construction of a new Luanda International Airport at Bom Jesus. Many of these project have been delayed (see below) and are still due to be completed.

CIF, a private Hong Kong-based institution, was meant to provide the funds to undertake these projects. According to a senior government official close to the presidency, GRN projects are valued at somewhere around $10 billion. In April 2007 the World Bank published an Angolan ministry of finance estimate of the loan as being $9.8 billion at Libor plus 1.5 per cent.[33] The US department of state 2008 'Investment climate statement' on Angola estimates the CIF loan figure at between $2.9 billion and $9 billion.[34] These figures broadly fall into the $10 billion figure mentioned by Chinese vice president Xi Jinping when he visited Luanda in 2011 (see above). However, according to the former Angolan ambassador in Beijing, João Manuel Bernardo, total credit lines from China to Angola for the purposes of national reconstruction stood at $6 billion in September 2010. The ambassador also stated that $2 billion from the 2004 credit line had already been used up.[35]

While there is uncertainty regarding the exact figures, it is also unclear how these funds were allocated across projects.

Throughout 2007 and for much of 2008 many GRN projects came to a standstill, provoking a lot of media speculation. Although it was reported that CIF had some difficulties in raising funds to complete the projects, a GRN technician admitted that a lack of planning on the part of GRN also contributed towards the failure of many construction projects even to start. As he explained: 'We went ahead with projects pressured by strict time deadline and did not take into account the forward planning that is required in a country like ours... We overlooked crucial elements such as the fact that our ports would not be able to cope with the increased amount of material being imported for these projects.'[36] Chinese construction firms also complained about CIF cajoling contractors into taking part in projects in Angola, routinely delaying payment for completed work and keeping rates as low as possible.[37] As a result, some of the funds from the second Exim Bank loan were used to continue the major programmes of GRN, but the ministry of finance was forced to raise $3.5 billion in domestic funding by issuing treasury bonds in 2007. This was a new departure as Angolan funds were being used for the first time to finance Chinese firms to ensure completion of these projects.

In May 2010 Manuel Hélder Vieira Dias 'Kopelipa', the former head of GRN, was replaced by President dos Santos with António Teixeira Flor, ex-vice minister of urbanism and housing. This was followed by a presidential decree in September 2010 which saw GRN disbanded and its various responsibilities redistributed. The development of the Luanda areas of Kilamba Kiaxi, Zango and Cacuaco were transferred from GRN to Sonangol Real Estate and Property (Sonangol Imobiliária e Propriedade – Sonip)[38] and the son of José Eduardo dos Santos, José Filomeno dos Santos 'Zenú', took over the oversight of the construction of the new airport. Despite the decentralisation of GRN there is, however, no indication that the control of core aspects of GRN has been ceded by the presidency.

CIF in Africa

China Sonangol, while still firmly entrenched in Angolan oil exploration, has diversified its business as well as its geographical radius of action. This has happened in conjunction with, and sometimes under the guise of, CIF.

Guinea

CIF reportedly has a $1.6 billion investment plan for Guinea. Target areas are the development of water and electricity infrastructure, urban housing development, mining, transport, tourism, as well as aquaculture and agriculture. Other projects relate to the creation of a joint venture for exploration in Guinea in partnership with Sonangol, the creation of an airline company, and the restoration of the airport, among others.

In October 2009 CIF agreed a $7 billion deal with the then military junta of Guinea, resulting in the Guinea Development Corporation (GDC) – a joint venture between the Guinean government, CIF and CSIH. The deal survived the political changes in Guinea and continues to stand as of March 2012. One of CIF's partners is the Australian mining company Bellzone. Former Guinean minister for mines, energy and hydraulics, and former senior vice president of UBS International (New York), Mahmoud Thiam, is intimately involved as director of GDC.

As part of this venture CIF was involved in restoring Guinean transport capabilities, notably restoring part of the Guinean rail network, and operating the newly formed Air Guinée International. CIF also is said to pay the salary of the coach of the Guinean national football team.

Zimbabwe

The Guinea deal was followed in November 2009 by China Sonangol agreeing a $8 billion deal with Mugabe's Zimbabwe – trading infrastructure in exchange for gold, platinum and oil concessions, oil and gas exploration, fuel procurement and distribution, and housing development. In Zimbabwe a new joint venture has been created to become part of the web of companies that also includes CIF and CSIH: Sino-Zim Development.

The announcement of this massive investment prompted the Chinese embassy in Harare to announce:

> The Chinese embassy certifies that China International Fund Ltd is an international company registered in Hong Kong. Its investment in Zimbabwe is completely its own corporate behavior. The Chinese government has nothing to do with its business operations. The embassy doesn't have any knowledge of the specifics.[39]

Diamonds are another target area for CSIH in Zimbabwe and the group has already mounted significant operations in the Marange diamond fields. This was confirmed by Manuel Vicente, former chief executive of Sonangol, on 24 February 2011 at a press conference in Luanda.[40]

Part of China Sonangol's plans for Zimbabwe include an upgrade to the Harare airport as well as a modernised Air Zimbabwe – the national carrier. Two Airbus 340 (Serial Number MSN 886 and 894) were delivered in June 2011 from Toulouse, France. According to the Zimbabwean newspaper the *Independent*, the aircraft, which cost around $200 million each, were bought using 'diamonds money' in a deal that was structured to bypass European Union- and US-imposed sanctions on Zimbabwe.[41]

Tanzania

China Sonangol also has been in long negotiations to take over the Tanzanian national carrier – Air Tanzania. An initial agreement of cooperation was made in 2006. This deal was also discussed in the 88 Queensway Group report by the US–China Economic and Security Review Commission, which stated that China Sonangol was granted three oil exploration licences in exchange for purchasing a 49 per cent share in Tanzania's national airline.[42]

While this project has been pronounced dead at many stages, there was still hope as late as July 2010.[43] In July 2010 in a feigned fit of desperation, Air Tanzania rejected China Sonangol and sought other partners. Notably, the partner of choice was Air Zimbabwe.[44] The Zimbabwean national carrier was at the time already in discussions to purchase the two aircraft mentioned above and must have already had an agreement with China Sonangol. Given these facts, rather than creating one of the biggest commercial agreements on African routes, the approach by Air Tanzania to cooperate with Air Zimbabwe must be seen as yet another attempt to get CSIH into Tanzania.

To their credit, Tanzanian parliamentarians argued that the deal between China Sonangol and Air Tanzania violated Tanzanian tender practice and thus also violated privatisation laws. As a result, in late 2010 more bidders were invited to join the privatisation process.

Mozambique

Through CIF, the CSIH conglomerate has entered Mozambique. CIF-MOZ is a joint venture consisting of CIF (80 per cent) and SPI Gestão e Investimentos SARL (20 per cent), which is the holding company of the ruling Frelimo party in Mozambique. CIF-MOZ is set to be active in agriculture, construction, manufacturing, mining, tourism and trade.

Projects underway already include a cement plant near Salamanga in Matutuine district south of Maputo, which has caused some consternation and anger amongst the local population to do with the relocation of around 230 families.[45] The plant cost around $72 million and will have the capacity to produce 5,000 tonnes of cement a day (1.8 million tonnes per year).

Madagascar

Since the coup that brought Andry Rajoelina to power in March 2009, Madagascar has been another focus of attention of the China Sonangol network. Like in Guinea and Zimbabwe, a joint venture – the Madagascar Development Corporation (MDC) – was established. This happened on 15 December 2010 between CIF (85 per cent) and Malagasy authorities (15 per cent). Focus areas include agriculture, industry, tourism and mining. Director of the GDC, Mahmoud Thiam, is said to be leading relations with Rajoelina.[46]

What are CSIH and CIF?

CIF was created in 2003 and appears to be the construction arm of Beiya International Development Ltd, a parent company of China Angola Oil Stock Holding Ltd, which trades Angolan oil and is linked to CSIH.

According to Sonangol, CSIH is a joint venture that 'was established in mid-2004 and has its HQ in Hong Kong'. Its business activity is 'exploration and production of oil and gas'. The CSIH website states that the company trades in crude oil and has oil blocks in Angola and 'the ultra-deep waters off Nigeria'.[47] According to the Hong Kong registry of companies, CSIH was set up in September 2004 and is 70 per cent beneficially owned by Beiya International Development and 30 per cent by Sonangol EP. New Bright appears to have taken over the share of Beiya, which has since renamed itself Dayuan.

CSIH is one of the many companies associated with the Angolan–Chinese joint venture and the Cayman Islands-registered SSI. The ownership of SSI changed in March 2010, when it was acquired by a subsidiary of Sinopec Corporation from a subsidiary of China Petrochemical Corporation (which is also the controlling stakeholder of Sinopec Corporation, with a 75.84 per cent share). It appears that SSI engages exclusively in deep-water acreage off Angola (exploration and production), while CSIH is active in shallow water/onshore as well as ultra-deep-water sites. As shown in the previous section, China Sonangol diversified its operations through the China International Fund (CIF). More information on the set-up of these and other related companies, as well as persons attached to these networks can be found in *Thirst for African Oil: Asian National Oil Companies in Nigeria and Angola*.[48]

Chinese officials have denied any link between CIF and the Chinese government but acknowledge that the company has contributed to the development of Angola.[49] Indeed, CIF's brand new skyscraper head office, the 25-floor CIF tower, dwarfs Angola's nearby national assembly building in central Luanda.

Chinese officials have distanced themselves from the company at various points. A spokesperson from the Chinese embassy in Angola said, 'We are not familiar with [CIF's] background, but all their projects have been built in Angola are not good,'[50] and a commercial counsellor from the Chinese embassy in Angola said, 'We are not the direct department in charge of Chinese–Angolan economic cooperative efforts, but we never saw [CIF] merge in any of the public exercises and meetings between the Chinese government and the Angolan government'.[51]

CIF seems to have successfully positioned itself between the Chinese and the Angolan governments (and between Sonangol and Sinopec) and controls access to Angolan resources. This is even the case for Angolan oil contracts for Sinopec – they are controlled by CIF.[52] CIF was able to get into this position by initially organising a team of four well-connected business people who were close to some Chinese government agencies. Through their connections the contracts kept coming, and CIF's position as the bridge to Angola became virtually unassailable.

The CSIH and CIF company web includes some illustrious personalities, and reaches into the highest echelons of the Angolan presidency. For example, José Filomeno dos Santos, the son of the president of Angola, is the official Sonangol representative at CSIH, and the CIF delegation to Guinea included Manuel Vicente – former CEO of Sonangol, step-nephew of the president of Angola and current minister for economic coordination in the Office of the Presidency.

Although the Sinopec Group has indicated that overseas operations will be transferred to its publicly listed subsidiary (Sinopec

Corporation), it has not added its Angolan equity production numbers to the latter's disclosures. To add to the confusion, in Angola's ministry of petroleum 'Report on petroleum sector activity in 2007' (published 11 June 2009), SSI (and CSIH) is referred to as a 'national, privately-owned oil company',[53] while at the same time it was reported on the Chinese National Development and Reform Commission website that 'the [Chinese central] government has approved Sinopec's $983 million acquisition in March [2011] for Total's 5 per cent stake in Angolan oil block 31 via China Sonangol International.'[54]

Far from being limited to Angola, CSIH and CIF are expanding into other African markets. The story seems to be the same everywhere. Upon news stories of Chinese investments into the country in question, the inevitable disclaimers that CSIH and CIF has nothing to do with the Chinese state follow from the Chinese embassies. The nature of CIF and CSIH only gets more complex instead of clearer the more one analyses it.

Conclusion

From both the Angolan and the Chinese perspective, this relationship is pragmatic and strategic. Chinese financing was provided when concessional funding was not available for Angola. Integral to this cooperation is China's need to access energy resources. In the construction sector, Angola is a particularly favourable market for many Chinese companies, which deliver quickly and have their risk mitigated by funding guarantees from the Chinese government, underpinned by oil-backed loans to Angola. Angola needs significant outside investment and there is relatively little competition. As a result, Chinese firms have found profitable deals, although they are now under increasing pressure to hire Angolans. Despite China's efforts to enter the oil sector, production is still dominated by Western companies.

For the Angolan government the relationship brings significant advantages to the country, helping to support economic growth. As a commodity-based economy emerging from 27 years of conflict, Angola was in desperate need of new partners and a new source of FDI. China provides a new model of cooperation, based on credit lines, economy and commerce, which contrasts with Western efforts of cooperation based on aid attached to conditionality.

The influence of China in Angola is often overplayed, and there is a growing fatigue among Angolan officials about the West's fixation with it.[55] For the most part, Angolan officials are open about their cooperation with China and candid about not wanting to depend on any one development or commercial partner. President dos Santos in his 2008 new year address to the diplomatic corps stressed that the Angolan government plans to reinforce its bilateral and commercial relationships with other countries: 'Globalisation naturally makes us see the need to diversify international relations and to accept the principle of competition, which has in a dynamic manner replaced the petrified concept of zones of influence that used to characterise the world.'[56]

This resonates well with Angola's stated desire to diversify its international and economic relations. India could be considered a natural partner in a multi-polar world. In fact, however, India has been the greatest loser to date with Indian companies being flat-footed in competition with China for oil concessions and unable to compete directly in cash terms.

The failure of Indian and other (including Chinese) companies to get a better foothold in Angola can be attributed to the dominance of Western oil companies, and the success of CSIH.

CSIH has prevented Chinese national oil companies from acquiring oil acreage in the past (see Marathon block 32 above) but has its influence in Angola peaked? The awards to it in the pre-salt round were limited and it looked as if a 25 per cent stake in block 31 (being relinquished by Exxon), could go to Indonesian state energy firm Pertamina, although Pertamina said in November 2011 that Angolan companies would get a right of first refusal and if that happened Pertamina would withdraw its $3.5 billion offer. Pertamina and China's CNOOC had considered a joint bid in May 2011 for Exxon's stake in block 31 but this failed and Pertamina bid alone. CNOOC and Pertamina have however 'declared interest' in a 10 per cent stake held by the US's Marathon in block 32. In both cases, Angola's state oil company will have the right of first refusal – if China Sonangol or its affiliates benefit it will indicate that this joint-venture vehicle continues to flourish as Angola's preferred oil partnership model with China. At the end of the day it is Angola's elite that calls the shots in deciding oil concessions, and their preference to date has been to channel Chinese engagement through China Sonangol.

Notes

1. Vines, A., Wong, L., Weimer, M. and Campos, I. (2009) *Thirst for African Oil: Asian National Oil Companies in Nigeria and Angola*, London, Chatham House.
2. 'Chinese imports of Iranian products soar', 26 July 2011, http://oilprice.com/Latest-Energy-News/Chinese-Imports-of-Iranian-Petroleum-Products-Soar.html, accessed 1 August 2011.
3. Global trade atlas (2011), FACTS Global Energy, EIA, in US Energy Information Administration (EIA) 2011, http: //www.eia.gov/countries/cab.cfm?fips=AO, accessed 28 November 2011.
4. *Jornal de Angola* (2006) 'PR defende cooperacao constutiva com a China', 21 June.
5. Banco Nacional de Angola (BNA), in African Development Bank (2011) *Angola 2011–2015, Country Strategy Paper and 2010 Country Portfolio Performance Review*, January: 5.
6. Angop (2007) 'Angolan leader addresses OPEC summit in Saudi Arabia', 19 November.
7. Macauhub (2011) 'Visit by "future leader of China" to Angola boosts bilateral relations', 31 January, http://macauhub.com.mo/en/2011/01/31/visit-by-%E2%9Cfuture-leader-of-china%E2%80%9D-to-angola-boosts-bilateral-relations, accessed 10 August 2011.
8. Foster, V. et al (2008) 'Building bridges: China's growing role as infrastructure financier for sub-Saharan Africa', World Bank and Public-Private Infrastructure Advisory Facility, July.
9. EIU, *Angola Monthly Report*, April 2008.
10. Serge, M. (2008) 'When China met Africa', *Foreign Policy* 166.
11. Radio Nacional de Angola, 'CFB estende rota ao Zimbabwe', July 2011.
12. According to the *Diaro da Republica* (State Gazette) 22(1), 21 February 2005, oil minister Desiderio da Graca Verissimo da Costa authorised the termination of the contract with Shell Development Angola BV for 50 per cent participation in the exploration of block 18, and authorised the same type of contract for Sonangol EP and Sinopec International through SSI. SSI would be responsible for the timetable of amortisations, reporting of damages and accountability of recovery costs.
13. According to the Chinese version of the CSIH website, SSI is responsible for the part of the business related to oil blocks in Angola, http://www.chinasonangol.com/chi/business.asp, accessed 5 April 2012.
14. This was oversubscribed as 40 banks replied.
15. Interview with BNP Paribas official, Paris, 10 March 2009.
16. *Trade Finance* (2005) 'Establishing new patterns of trade', 1 December 2005.
17. *Africa Energy Intelligence* (2005) 'The Angola–China connection', 27 July.
18. When Total's PSA expired on 30 June 2005 it was not renewed.

19. Manuel Vicente, former president of Sonangol, signed the agreement In Beijing in mid 2005.
20. *Shanghai Securities News* (2006) 'China's Sinopec wins bid for stakes in Angola oil blocks', 13 June.
21. In block 18/06, Brazil's Petrobas was awarded the operatorship of the block with a smaller share than its main equity partner on the block, SSI, which secured a 40 per cent stake.
22. *Africa Energy Intelligence*, 18 June 2008.
23. http:www.streetinsider.com/Corporate+News/Marathon+Oil+(MRO)+to+Sell+Interest+in+Block+32+Offshore+Angola+fpr+$1.3+Billion/4800732.html, accessed 30 July 2009.
24. Form 10-Q, Quarterly report pursuant to Section 13 or 15(D) of the Securities Exchange Act of 1934, for the quarterly period ended June 30, 2011, Commission file number 1-5153, Marathon Oil Corporation http://www.sec.gov/Archives/edgar/data/101778/000010177811000048/form10q2011aug8.htm, accessed 22 March 2012
25. Universo, Sonangol, June 2010: 37, https://www.sonangol.co.ao/wps/wcm/connect/793f2980475d5edaa7cbff7c37a37d2d/SU26+web.pdf?MOD=AJPERES, accessed 22 March 2012
26. Reuters (2008) 'China eyes more loans for cash-tight Angola', 19 December.
27. *Xinhua* (2009) 'China, Angola discuss China's new credit line of over $1bn', 12 March.
28. Angop (2008) 'Govt, China Development Bank analyse cooperation', 24 September.
29. *China Daily* (2009) 'Mutual growth marks Sino-Angolan partnership', 22 January. Gou Jiang is also vice chair of the China Development Bank.
30. Angop (2009) 'Head of state, Chinese ambassador discuss cooperation', 17 February.
31. The Angolan vice minister for external relations, Exalgina Gamboa, and Chinese vice minister for commerce, Jiang Zengwei.
32. Interview with Chinese official, Luanda, 4 March 2009.
33. World Bank, 'International Development Association interim strategy note for the Republic of Angola', Report No. 39394-AO, 26 April 2007, Annex 7: 'Non-concessional borrowing by government of Angola since 2004', p.49. This reports that there were also three months' management commission at 0.3 per cent and immobilisation commission, also at 0.3 per cent.
34. US Department of State (2008), '2008 investment climate statement – Angola', http://www.state.gov/e/eeb/ifd/2008/100819.htm, accessed 1 August 2011.
35. In AngolaPress 23 September 2010, http://www.minfin.gov.ao/NoticiaD.aspx?Codigo=10501, accessed 1 August 2011.
36. Interview, Luanda 3 October 2007.
37. *Asia Times Online* (2007) 'China's stock bubble can be traced to Angola', 27 March.
38. SONIP is a 20 per cent shareholder of newly formed Mota-Engil Angola (other shareholders include Mota-Engil 51 per cent, Banco Privado

Atlantico (BPA) 11 per cent and Finicapital Globalpactum 18 per cent).

39. *Xinhua* (2009) 'Embassy says China International Fund Ltd a HK firm', 30 December, http://www.chinadaily.com.cn/china/2009-12/30/content_9249034.htm, accessed 8 March 2012.

40. *Africa–Asia Confidential* 4(6) (2011) 'Sino-Zimbabwe in the Marange diamond fields'.

41. *The Independent* (Zimbabwe) (2011) 'Chinese in deal to save Air Zim', 20 April, http://www.zimbabwesituation.com/apr22a_2011.htm# Z2, accessed 3 August 2011.

42. Levkowitz, L., Ross, M.M. and Warner, J.R. (2009) 'The 88 Queensway Group: a case study in Chinese investors' operations in Angola and beyond', Washington, US–China Economic and Security Review Commission, http://www.uscc.gov/The_88_Queensway_Group.pdf, accessed 12 April 2012

43. *Africa–Asia Confidential* 3(9) (2010) 'Choose your poison'.

44. *The East African* (2010), 'Air Tanzania ditches Chinese firm and partners with Air Zimbabwe', 5 July, http://www.theeastafrican.co.ke/business/-/2560/951808/-/3ubpiqz/-/index.html, accessed 3 August 2011.

45. *Savana* (2011) 'Populaçã revoltada com a cimenteira de Matutuine', June 17.

46. Other countries where CIF and/or CSIH are active, but which were excluded from this chapter due to lack of resources, include Democratic Republic of Congo (DRC) and Nigeria.

47. See www.sonangol.com and www.chinasonangol.com, which post an archive of 'CIF News'.

48. Vines et al (2009) *Thirst for African Oil: Asian National Oil Companies in Nigeria and Angola*, London, Chatham House.

49. *First Finance Daily* (2007) 'Dan Yinmu speaks for the first time; Chinese embassy in Angola is not familiar with CIF background', 29 March.

50. Zong Xinjian and Lu Yuan, 'Dan Yinmu shou du kai kou: Zhongguo zhu an shi guan bu liao jie Zhong ji bei jing' ('Dan Yinmu speaks for the first time; Chinese embassy in Angola is not familiar with CIF background'), *First Finance Daily*, 29 March 2007 (USCC staff translation), http://finance.sina.com.cn/g/20070329/02383450690.shtml, in Levkowitz, Ross and Warner, 'The 88 Queensway Group': 23.

51. Ibid.

52. CIF maintains an oil department in Shanghai, where it holds regular training workshops.

53. http://www.minpet.gov.ao/PublicacoesD.aspx?Codigo=477, accessed 8 March 2012.

54. 'China approves Sinopec investments in Indonesia, Angola oil, gas fields' Singapore (Platts) 2 August 2011/218 http://www.platts.com/RSSFeedDetailedNews/RSSFeed/Oil/7099498, accessed 10 August 2011.

55. Interview with José Pedro de Morais, finance minister, Luanda, 13 October 2007.

56. Luanda, 10 January 2008.

6

Taming the dragon: China's oil interests in Angola

Ana Cristina Alves

Introduction

Angola–China diplomatic ties date back to 1983, but the relationship remained dormant in the following two decades. Angola–China relations only flourished at the start of the 21st century, within the context of emerging economic complementarities. The growing financial power of Beijing and its thirst for markets and natural resources led to the internationalisation of the Chinese economy at the turn of the century. This coincided with the end of the civil war in Angola in 2002, the need for national reconstruction and the increase in petroleum production. The synergies generated within this context largely justified the dramatic expansion of bilateral relations seen in the last decade.

The new phase in this relationship had been marked by the intensification of political and economic interchanges. Contrasting sharply with the previous decades, high-level official visits became increasingly frequent in both directions, culminating in the signature of a strategic partnership agreement at the end of 2010.

However, the tightening of this political partnership is a direct consequence of the dynamism of economic relations throughout the past decade. Since the end of the civil war in Angola, China has played an increasingly relevant role as a development partner, particularly via subsidies for the construction of public buildings and cooperation programmes within the areas of health, education and agriculture. The most significant characteristic of the relationship, however, is the rapid increase in the volume of bilateral trade, clearly dominated by petroleum exports to China. In addition, China has played a prominent role in the reconstruction and rehabilitation of the country's infrastructures by extending large concessional lines of credit.

Coming from a fairly gloomy historical context, in under a decade China has managed to achieve a prominent position in Angola's economy, namely as its major commercial partner, an important source of funds and as a major operator in the country's reconstruction projects. Although barely evident at first glance, a closer look will reveal that the petroleum factor has facilitated all aspects of China's economic commitment in Angola: bilateral trade is dominated by petroleum imports, lines of credit for infrastructure construction are repaid in oil, and the largest chunk of Chinese investment in the country is intended for the hydrocarbon industry.

Since 2007 Beijing has been the main destination for Angolan petroleum exports – almost 40 per cent of exports in 2010 – and Angola has become the second largest supplier of petroleum to China, after Saudi Arabia, with whom it has been vying for first place for the past three years.

Having moved from self-sufficiency to becoming the second largest importer and consumer of petroleum worldwide in less than two decades, China has significantly increased its vulnerability to international market fluctuations. Beijing has therefore sought to increase its external reserves with the objective of ensuring a continuous supply to the greatest extent possible. Within this context, and as its second largest supplier, the Angolan petroleum industry has special relevance in China's strategy. Beijing's interests in Angola have been pursued by the Sinopec Group (China Petrochemical Corporation), the second largest Chinese petroleum company.

Sonangol Sinopec International – the wedding and the honeymoon

The Chinese national oil company, Sinopec, acquired shares in its first petroleum block in Angola soon after the signature by the Angolan government of the first line of credit from the Chinese Export and Import Bank (Exim Bank) in March 2004. The plot acquired refers to 50 per cent of block 18, operated by British Petroleum (50 per cent). The surrounding framework and the procedures adopted in the acquisition process are proof of the crucial role played by the extension of the loan and the resultant connections at the highest level. The block in question belonged to Shell which, allegedly, owing to the increased cost of exploration and the low success rate with regard to the volume of reserves discovered, put it on sale in mid-2003. In April 2004, Shell came to an agreement to sell its shares to the national Indian petroleum company – Oil and Natural Gas Company (ONGC) (*Africa–Asia Confidential* 2009).

From the middle of 2003, the Angolan government found itself in negotiations with Exim Bank for the first tranche of the $2 billion credit line, in which Sonangol played a central role as guarantor and responsible party for repayment of the loan.

In the middle of 2004, it became clear that Sonangol was going to exercise its preferential right on block 18 to prevent the transaction with ONGC, by virtue of Sinopec being willing to pay more for Shell shares – $725. The objective of the Angolan government was to explore the block in question in partnership with Sinopec (*Semanário Angolense* 2004). To this end, in September 2004 a joint venture was set up between Sonangol and a subsidiary of the Sinopec Group (Sinopec Overseas Oil & Gas, SOOG) giving birth to Sonangol Sinopec International (SSI).

In December 2004 Sonangol formally exercised its preferential right to purchase Shell's shareholding of 50 per cent in block 18. Confirming the goodwill generated by China in the upper echelons of the Angolan political elite, the minister of petroleum at that time, Desidério Costa, formally sanctioned the transfer of the block in question to SSI in February 2005 (Angop 2005a). In this way SSI assumed control of the above-mentioned plot of block 18 in terms of the pre-existing production sharing agreement (PSA).

It is interesting to note that, via this joint venture, Sinopec also developed links with a private Chinese investment fund associated with Sonangol. The intricate personal network behind this fund connects the top echelons of the Angolan elite, via Sonangol, with a Chinese private capital group with its headquarters in Hong Kong. This is the same group which, in 2005, started to channel funds for the construction of infrastructures in Angola via the controversial China International Fund (CIF).

Sonangol formally partnered with this private Chinese fund in June 2004, through Sonangol Asia,[1] (see figure 6.1). In August 2004, China Sonangol International Holding Ltd (CSHI) was created – commonly referred to as China Sonangol – with the objective of increasing the group's energy projects in Angola, and facilitating Sonangol's access to funding. Dayuan International Development Ltd, the core company in this Chinese private capital fund, holds 70 per cent of the capital of China Sonangol with the remaining 30 per cent belonging to Sonangol. The Sinopec group, through the subsidiary SOOG, formally partnered with this private fund through its majority shareholding in Sonangol Sinopec International, where it holds a 55 per cent share. Dayuan International Development Ltd holds a share of 31.5 per cent and China Sonangol the remaining 13.5 per cent (Vines et al 2009). Despite Dayuan formally owing a larger shareholding of SSI, it was from the start managed by Luanda as a joint venture between Sonangol and Sinopec

Some time after the acquisition of 50 per cent of block 18 by SSI, the Chinese deputy prime minister paid a three-day visit to Luanda (25–27 February 2005), during which time he held private meetings, firstly with President José Eduardo dos Santos and then with the minister of petroleum, Desidério Costa, and the chairman of Sonangol, Manuel Vicente. Zeng Peiyang also coordinated with the Angolan prime minister, Fernando da Piedade Dias dos Santos, the signature of nine cooperation agreements, five intergovernmental and four corporate (Angop 2005b). Four of the five intergovernmental agreements and three of the four corporate agreements were related to energy. The intergovernmental agreements included an agreement for closer cooperation in energy, mining and infrastructures, a memorandum of understanding to create a bilateral commission, and two cooperation agreements between the National Development and Reform Commission (NDRC, the political nucleus for development policy coordination in China), the ministry of petroleum and the ministry of geology and mines. Within the scope of the corporate agreements, Sonangol signed a long-term supply contract with Sinopec, and the two companies also signed a memorandum to study joint exploration of block 3/80[2] and to jointly develop the Lobito-Sonaref refinery project (Angop 2005b).

Figure 6.1 Sonangol Sinopec International in the Hong Kong group structure

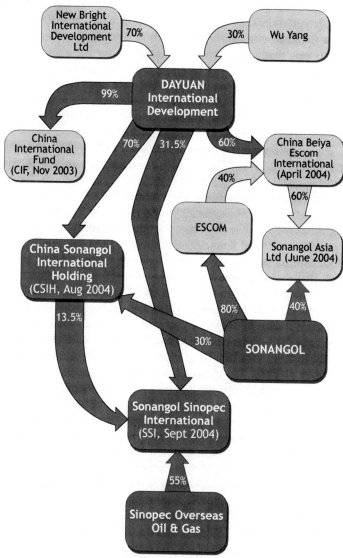

Source: adapted from diagrams in Levkowitz et al (2009), Vines et al (2009) and interview with Angolan sector analyst (1 Feb 2011)

The long-term petroleum supply project signed between Sinopec and Sonangol – for a seven-year period at 40,000 barrels per day (bpd) for the first three years – enabled Sonangol to fund Angolan offshore exploration projects during the summer of 2005. Via a financial engineering manoeuvre designed by the Calyon Investment Bank, the recently created China Sonangol (CSIH) became the debtor (*Energy Compass* 2009), Sinopec the guarantor and Unipec – the Sinopec trading wing – the underwriter. Calyon Bank advanced an initial sum of $2 billion and via a syndicated loan – where there was excess demand – Sonangol met the amount of $3 billion (*Africa Intelligence* 2005).

The same financial expedient was used in May 2006 to obtain $1.4 billion on behalf of Sonangol Sinopec International with the objective of developing its shareholding in block 18, having attracted the interest of numerous international and Chinese banks[3] (*Trade and Finance Magazine* 2007). As seen in a Chatham House report, it was the first time that the Sinopec group had used this type of international financial instrument to fund the development of its foreign petroleum assets. Moreover, as mentioned by the study, the dynamic generated by the acquisition of the shareholding in block 18 benefited China in two ways. Firstly, it facilitated access to the new petroleum exploration technologies via a close partnership with BP – its sole partner in the block – and, secondly, it became the recipient of the majority of the petroleum produced by SSI in this block by virtue of the petroleum-guaranteed loans (Vines et al 2009). The close relationship that Sinopec established in this way with Sonangol thus benefited the interests of Sinopec in the hydrocarbon sector in Angola in an initial phase. China's increased financial capacity and the fact that Sinopec was in the good graces of the Angolan elite largely explained the expansion of China's petroleum assets in the following year. Although the 3/80 block – later classified as 3/05 and 3/05A – had not been awarded to Sinopec but to China Sonangol[4] (Vines et al 2009: 44), the Chinese group acquired, through SSI, important assets in the tender that took place between November 2005 and May 2006. During the tender round in question, SSI acquired three shareholdings in some of the most disputed blocks of ultra-deep water – 20 per cent in block 15/06, operated by ENI; 27.5 per cent in block 17/06, managed by Total; and 40 per cent in block 18/06, operated by Petrobras.

Based on its effective share in block 18 (27.5 per cent), the estimated petroleum production volume of Sinopec in Angola is 44,000 bpd (see table 6.1).[5] Block 18, which is 5,000km^2, is divided into east and west zones, with the former containing one of the most promising fields, Plutónio, which started production in October 2007 (Scandinavian Oil and Gas 2010). With estimated reserves of over 500 million barrels and potential production of 240,000 bpd, based on the grouping of various fields, block 18 represented 10.5 per cent of Angolan petroleum exports in 2010 – the fifth largest in Angola (Ministry of Finance of Angola 2010). The Grande Plutónio zone has an anticipated production life of 20–21 years, and it is expected to generate $63 billion in revenue between 2010–27 (Sunita 2010). This asset signifies a potential increase of 8.8 per cent – 72,520 bpd – in Sinopec's daily foreign petroleum production, as well as 3.6 per cent – 102 million barrels – of its proven reserves. The west zone is still in the development phase. When the blocks acquired in 2006 – blocks 15/06, 17/06 and 18/06, whose combined reserve potential is estimated at 3.2 billion barrels (Agência Lusa 2006) – start production (2014–18), Sinopec's petroleum production in Angola may exceed 100,000 bpd.

Lobito refinery and the souring of relations

The honeymoon between the Angolan and Chinese petroleum companies was, however, short. Sonangol-Sinopec relations suffered an initial backslide during the 2006 tender, following which there was a misunderstanding over the signature bonus. On the brink of bid submission, SSI realised, through contacts in petroleum circles in Luanda, that the bonuses should be much higher than expected and, knowing Sinopec's interest in acquiring shares, alerted the latter to this fact. When the bids were known, Sinopec realised that its offers had exceeded the highest by about $150 million. Unhappy about this fact, the Chinese state company pressurised Sonangol to lower its bonuses to the highest value offered by other companies. Discontent with the growing pressure from the Chinese side, Sonangol temporarily moved its assets to China Sonangol and invited other companies to take on the plots in question. Faced with the prospect of the imminent loss of these assets, Sinopec took the bonuses and the assets were once again

Table 6.1 Sonangol Sinopec International petroleum assets in Angola

Asset	Consortium	Estimated reserves* (barrels)	Known investment
50% block 18 2004	BP [Op] 50%	1 billion	$1.4 billion
20% block 15/06 2006	ENI [Op] 35%; Sonangol E.P. 15%; Total 15%; Falcon Oil 5%; Gemas 5%	1.5 billion	Total SB: $902 million, Total CB: $50 million, SSI Quota**: SB: $207 million, CB: $12 million
27.5% block 17/06 2006	Total [Op] 26%; Sonangol E.P. 24%; Falcon Oil 5%; ACR 5%; Partex 2.5%; Somoil 10%	1 billion	Total SB: $1.1 billion, SSI Quota: SB: $398 million, CB: $32 million
40% block 18/06 2006	Petrobras [Op] 30%; Sonangol E.P. 20%; Falcon Oil 5%; Gemas 5%	700 million	Total SB $1.1 billion, SSI Quota: SB: $540million, CB: $50 million
Estimated total	–	–	$2.64 thousand million (approx.)

SB: Signature bonus
CB: Corporate bonus

* Potential estimates of reserves by operators, Sonangol and others.

** All parties have to pay the equivalent of the respective share in the block plus Sonangol's share, which is divided among all.

moved to SSI.[6] According to Wood Mackenzie, the bids offered during this round were at that time the highest ever offered for petroleum assets (Reed 2006). The tender level was involuntarily inflated by Sinopec, who allegedly offered $2.2 billion in signature bonuses for the acquisition of blocks 17/06 and 18/06.

Some time after the tender round, the deputy prime minister, Wen Jiabao, visited Angola (20–21 June 2006). In accordance with one of the agreements signed in 2005 (Agência Lusa 2005) and as

Production phase, depth and grade of crude	Total production 2009	Estimated liquid quota of Sinopec 2009***
Production (Plutónio, start Oct 2007); Deep water (1,200–1,500m); Light crude (33.2 API)	160,000 bpd	27.5% (44,000 bpd)
Exploration (Cabaça south, Oct 2010); Deep water (400–1,500m); Light crude (34 API)	–	11%
Exploration (Begonia, Apr 2010); Deep water (600–1,900m); Light crude (36 API)	–	15.3%
Exploration (Magnesium-01, Nov 2009); Deep water (750–1,750 m); Light crude (20 API)	–	22%
–	–	Reserves: 972 million barrels, production 44,000 bpd

*** This value is merely indicative given that the final volume of petroleum barrels varies according to the petroleum profit margin which is due to the government, and which differs depending on the petroleum price.

Sources: Ministry of Petroleum of Angola, Africa Energy Intelligence; EIA; Sonangol; ENI; Total; Petrobras; various reports (Upstream online, Offshore, Petróleo e Gás [Petroleum and Gas], Bloomberg, etc).

one of the prerequisites at the time for the acquisition of shares in blocks 15/06, 16/06 and 18/06, the chairman of Sonangol and the vice chairman of Sinopec signed a partnership agreement on 16 March 2006 for the construction of a refinery in Lobito. Negotiations on the project details started shortly thereafter. The refinery had long been on the Angolan government's agenda, since Angola imports over 70 per cent of its refined fuel (*Sonangol Universo* 2010: 39). Angola only has a small refinery located in Luanda which presently operates at half its capacity – 65,000 bpd – with this production being largely insufficient to supply the rapidly expanding domestic market.

The Lobito refinery (Sonaref), in which Sonangol would retain a shareholding of 70 per cent and Sinopec the remaining 30 per cent, was planned to have a processing capacity of 200,000 bpd, with the start of operations scheduled for 2010. At the time, the project was valued at $3.5 billion, the second largest project after the natural gas liquefaction plant in Soyo at $5 billion.

In this new agreement, Sinopec would advance the funding for the entire project. Despite the favourable context set by previous joint projects and the political capital which Sinopec clearly enjoyed in the Angolan executive,[7] the negotiations came to an impasse in January 2007 and the project collapsed in February 2007. At the time, newspapers reported the cause of the impasse as being a high level of disagreement related to the definition of the target market. In a press conference held on 23 February, the president publicly justified: 'we have come to a point were we cannot make concessions – we cannot build a refinery to produce for the Chinese market.' (Neto 2007)

However, interviews conducted by the author in China as well as Angola indicated a greater complexity with regard to the causes of the misunderstanding.[8] More specifically, the point of disagreement was the technology to be used that, owing to the different specifications in Asia and in the West, would limit export markets from the outset. While Beijing would want to supply the Chinese market, Luanda's aim was to supply its own domestic market and Western markets – the US and Europe. From the Angolan perspective, the profit margin would be much lower with production being exported to Asia, not only owing to the transport costs over long distances but also to the fact that the fuel is highly subsidised in most Asian markets, including China. In contrast, exports to Western markets immediately guarantees higher profit margins, owing to the geographical proximity and higher fuel prices in these markets, which to a certain degree counterbalances the fact that prices are subsidised in Angola.

Some interviewees also pointed out the location of the Lobito refinery as problematic as there were serious technological and logistical challenges as well as the disputable profitability of this project in the context of the international refining market. This perspective is corroborated by the fact that no other investor came forward to assist Sonangol in funding this project[9] despite all the efforts made by this state company and the favourable context of increased petroleum prices.

Some other interviewees emphasised the fact that this refinery was never a priority for Sinopec in Angola, making this a compromise just to please the Angolan government, which had linked the refinery project to the concession of blocks to be acquired in the 2005–06 tender process.

The alleged limited interest of Sinopec would have decreased during the negotiations owing to the narrowing of the prospect of profit, given that Sonangol planned to construct a highly sophisticated refinery with technology that Sinopec does not have at its disposal. This fact would substantially inflate the project cost and would make it unviable from the outset for Sinopec to contract its subsidiaries in favour of Western companies. Within this context, the negotiation would be less advantageous to Sinopec as it planned to capitalise not only on marketing of the products but on loan interest and project construction.[10] Sinopec, however, underestimated the impact that this episode would have on the expansion of its petroleum interests in Angola, especially in a context of increased petroleum prices.

The divorce and attempt at reconciliation

In the face of this unexpected obstacle, the Sinopec group made an effort to expand its petroleum assets in Angola outside the joint venture with Sonangol. Just a few months after the collapse of the partnership for Sonaref, Sinopec participated alone in the tender round for new blocks opening up at the end of that year (2007). The list of pre-qualified companies in this round included Sinopec International Group (as the operator) as well as SSI (as the non-operator).[11] However, the round was frozen in the middle of 2008, initially owing to the proximity of the legislative elections (September 2008) and afterwards owing to the global economic crisis.

At the end of 2008, Sinopec made another attempt to acquire petroleum assets in Angola separately from Sonangol. To this end, it joined forces with another Chinese petroleum company, China

National Offshore Oil Corporation (CNOOC), to acquire a 20 per cent shareholding in block 32 – ultra-deep water[12] – operated by Total. The share in question was put up for sale by Marathon within the context of the international financial crisis. The joint bid by Sinopec and CNOOC of $1.3 billion exceeded the rival bids of ONGC, Petrobras and even that of the other Chinese petroleum company, China National Petroleum Corporation (CNPC). The final agreement between Sinopec and CNOOC and Marathon was reached in July 2009 and it was hoped that the negotiation would be concluded before the end of the year (Marathon 2009). Meanwhile, in September 2009, Sonangol made public its intention to exercise its preferential right (Faucon 2009) thus blocking access by the Chinese consortium to this asset.

Sonangol's intervention would allegedly be based on market considerations, since the shareholding was being sold at a price lower than its real value – estimated at $1.4 billion–$1.6 billion by Goldman Sachs. Whether Sonangol's intervention was a consequence of Sinopec's withdrawal from the Sonaref project in 2007, or whether it was merely a decision taken to protect the market and avoid the drop in prices of its petroleum assets,[13] is still unclear.[14] Nevertheless, it is important to note that there has been a clear change in the relationship between Sonangol and Sinopec since that episode. If in 2004 Sonangol used its preferential right to benefit Sinopec, the same expedient was used here to prevent the acquisition of assets directly by Chinese companies. Sonangol's attitude is even more striking if we take into consideration the context of the economic crisis and the extremely weak financial situation in which Angola found itself at the time. Sonangol bought Marathon's 20 per cent shareholding in February 2010 for $1.3 billion, with the objective of selling it for a higher price when the market was more favourable (Upstream 2010). In the meanwhile the asset has been placed under China Sonangol.

Efforts made by Sinopec during the 2007–09 period to expand its assets in the Angolan petroleum industry separately from Sonangol were therefore unproductive, contrasting sharply with the previous period (2004–06), during which the ties between the two state companies were full steam ahead.

In March 2010, Sinopec International – the listed arm of the Sinopec group – acquired from the mother company – China

Petrochemical Corporation – the 55 per cent shareholding in SSI, thus replacing Sinopec Overseas Oil and Gas (SOOG). The deal totalled $2.5 billion (Scandinavian Oil and Gas 2010). This transaction clearly indicated Sinopec's desire to rehabilitate the joint venture with Sonangol, replacing SOOG – a subsidiary of the Sinopec group registered in the Cayman Islands – with another company in the group with a higher profile and a listing in the Hong Kong stock exchange.

Sinopec's reorganisation exercise took place at the same time as negotiations between Luanda and Beijing for the extension of new lines of credit. Although it is not clear to what extent these two events were coordinated, they indicated China's return to the same formula that had been so successful in 2004 – the quest for a closer partnership both with the Angolan executive and Sonangol, with the aim of improving its prospects in the Angolan petroleum industry.

The dynamic between Sonangol, SSI and China Sonangol

China Sonangol seems to have been the major beneficiary of the souring of relations between Sonangol and Sinopec. Contrasting sharply with the frustrated attempts by Sinopec in recent years, China Sonangol saw its petroleum asset collection growing in 2010–11 (see table 6.2), one part of which was directly to the detriment of Sinopec – Marathon's 20 per cent shareholding in block 32.

In addition, China Sonangol was listed as one of the winners of the first round of licensing for the pre-salt area of Angola (Faucon and Ordonez 2011) having been conceded, in January 2011, shareholdings in four of the eleven blocks on offer – blocks 19, 20, 36 and 38.

Neither SSI nor Sinopec featured among the companies selected by Sonangol for the pre-salt tender. Moreover, China Sonangol was the only company without relevant experience in the pre-salt invited to take part in this tender round, which once again confirms the crucial importance of alliance with Sonangol in order to prosper in the sector.

Most of the two companies' assets are, however, still in the exploration phase. Only block 05/03 (China Sonangol) and block 18 (SSI) are currently in production – 48,000 bpd and 160,000 bpd

Table 6.2 Petroleum assets of China Sonangol (CSIH) and Sonangol Sinopec International (SSI)

	Acquisition year	Depth
China Sonangol		
25% block 3/05A, 25% block 3/05	2006 (tender round)	Shallow water
5% block 31 (TEPA), 20% block 32 (Marathon)	2010 (shareholding put up for sale)	Ultra-deep water
10% block 19, 10% block 20, 20% block 36, 15% block 38	2011 (tender round)	Pre-salt
SSI		
50% block 18 (Shell)	2004 (shareholding put up for sale)	Deep water
20% block 15/06, 27.5% block 17/06	2006 (tender round)	
40% block 18/06		

SOURCE: Sonangol concession map (July 2011); for blocks acquired in 2011 interview, Luanda, 3 February 2011

Table 6.3 Angola – China Sonangol and SSI Exports

	China Sonangol		SSI		Total Angolan exports	
	Barrels '000	$ '000	Barrels '000	$ '000	Barrels '000	$ '000
2006	1.97	128,022	0	0	495,919	30,393,320
2007	2,955	210,643	3,924	339,664	605,482	42,357,156
2008	985	115,537	25,581	2,430,181	675,024	62,401,503
2009	1,969	143,519	25,851	1,607,896	646,938	39,219,541
2010	2,891	227,309	23,886	1,826,066	624,401	48,656,445

SOURCE: Angolan ministry of Petroleum (2010 and 2011) Report on the petroleum sector for 2009 July 2010, August 2011

respectively in 2009 (Ministry of Petroleum 2010:15). In terms of production, according to data from the Angolan ministry of petroleum (Ministry of Petroleum 2010:15), SSI is ranked seventh out of 21 companies exporting Angolan petroleum.

As seen in table 6.3, in spite of the setback in recent years with regard to new acquisitions, Sinopec currently has more petroleum in its operations in Angola than China Sonangol. Sinopec owes this fact to the first asset that it acquired in Angola, in block 18, within the context of the first line of credit extended by Exim Bank.

Conclusion

Having correctly identified infrastructure construction as a prime requirement for post-conflict Angola, Beijing offered its services in funding the Angolan government's reconstruction programme in exchange for preferential access to petroleum assets and long-term petroleum supplies.

Following the example of success stories in other African countries, the Chinese strategy for the acquisition of blocks went via the development of a close association with the political elite and with the Angolan NOC. In only two years (2004–06), Sinopec, through the partnership with Sonangol (SSI) accumulated a reserve potential of almost a billion barrels in some of the most promising deep-water blocks.

The poor management of the Sonaref episode by the Chinese state company, however, wiped out a future that appeared auspicious at that time. Based on its status as majority shareholder in the joint venture (SSI) and its elevated financial capacity, Sinopec clearly over-valued its ascendancy over Sonangol and underestimated the latter's ability to negotiate, primarily in the episode of the signature bonus, and afterwards in the Lobito refinery project. Sinopec's mismanagement of the relationship led to alienation of the Sonangol partnership, resulting in the frustrating attempts to expand Sinopec's interests on its own behalf in an industry largely controlled by the Angolan state company, since it also acts as the regulator for the oil industry.

In spite of its financial power, Sinopec has no mastery of technology related to exploration, development and production in ultra-deep water, where the large part of Angolan reserves are located. For this reason, and because there is a high level of competition in the Angolan industry between international petroleum companies who are masters of this technology, Sonangol's leverage proved to be greater than calculated by Sinopec initially.

The above analysis also reveals an interesting Sonangol–SSI–China Sonangol dynamic. Whenever misunderstandings arise between Sinopec and Sonangol, the blocks are temporarily transferred to China Sonangol – as demonstrated in the bonus and Sonaref episodes – and when resolved, the assets return to SSI. Rumour in Luanda has it that SSI may access China Sonangol shareholdings in block 32 and the pre-salt blocks if relations with the Angolan NOC warm up again. In the end, this strategy has proven to be fairly efficient for the Angolan state in pursing the interests of their NOC, which thus remains the strongest partner in this relationship.

With no new licensing round planned in the near future – unlikely owing to the large investments needed for exploration in the pre-salt and with Sonangol blocking its attempts to acquire assets for sale – Sinopec appears to have finally understood the game logic in Angola. The latest developments indicate that Beijing has returned to the formula implemented originally – based on solid intergovernmental relations and the consolidation of the partnership with Sonangol. This is illustrated by Sinopec's attempt to revitalise the partnership with Sonangol via the cosmetic change of ownership of its 55 per cent shareholding in SSI and by the extension of new lines of credit for infrastructure totalling $4.5 billion, most of which are to be guaranteed by petroleum.

From its side, the Angolan government has shown that it wants to separate Chinese credit lines from preferential access to oil assets. Attesting to this is the fact that Sinopec has failed to acquire new shareholdings in the Angolan hydrocarbon industry despite the extension of the new loans.

Developments over the last couple of years have clearly demonstrated that Sinopec has only one viable way of expanding its interests in the Angolan oil industry. This is via the partnership with Sonangol, which perceives SSI as an instrument to place the massive resources of the Chinese NOC at the service of Angolan interests.

An earlier version of this chapter was published in Portuguese in the report 'Energy in Angola in 2011', published by the Center for Studies and Scientific Research (CEIC) at the Catholic University of Angola (UCAN) in October 2011.

Notes

1. Through the establishment of a joint venture: Sonangol Asia Ltd, whose ownership capital comes 40 per cent from Sonangol and 60 per cent from China Beiya Escom International (the latter is owned 40 per cent by ESCOM and 60 per cent by Dayuan International Development). See Figure 6.1.
2. Block 3/80 was operated by Total and Sonangol did not intend to renew the contract, which expired in 2005 owing to the 'Angolagate' case, the protagonists of which, under sentence in France, had close ties with the Angolan executive.
3. Agricultural Bank of China, Bank of China, Bayern LB, BNP Paribas, Calyon, China Construction Bank, China Development Bank, China Exim Bank, ING Bank, KBC Finance, Natixis, SG CIB.
4. After the visit of Manuel Vicente to Beijing at the beginning of July 2005, these plots (25 per cent of block 3/05 and 25 per cent of block 3/05A, both operated by Sonangol E.P.) were conceded to China Sonangol. In 2007 these shareholdings were, for a brief period, handed over to SSI.
5. Technical problems with FPSO Grande Plutónio lowered production in 2010, estimated at approximately 90,000 bpd.
6. Interview by the author with Angolan oil sector analyst, 1 February 2011, Luanda, Angola.
7. According to several media reports, the Angolan political elite would prefer to sign the agreement with Sinopec instead of ONGC which was also tendering for this project.
8. Various interviews, public and private sector, Luanda, Angola, January–March 2008 and March 2009, and in China and Macau, October–December 2007.
9. In the context of increased petroleum revenue (pre-crisis), the Angolan government decided to go ahead alone with the Sonaref project. At the end of 2008, the technical implementation of the project was awarded to an American company, Kellogg Brown & Root (KBR). The cost of the project went up to $8,000 million, with the same production capacity (200,000 bpd) scheduled to begin in 2015.
10. Interview by the author with Angolan oil sector analyst, 1 February 2011, Luanda, Angola.
11. The list of pre-qualified companies is available on Sonangol's website: http://www.sonangol.co.ao, accessed 8 February 2011.
12. A promissory investment with estimated reserves of 1,500 million of light crude.

13. Interview by the author with Angolan private international law firm, 17 March 2009, Luanda, Angola.
14. Based on interviews conducted in Luanda (March 2009), and reports in the media, there seems to be a dividing line between government officials or persons close to the executive and civil society with respect to the change in the relationship between Sonangol and Sinopec. The first group denies any political change and reinforces market considerations in the decision-making process while the second group clearly sees a souring of relations further to the Sonaref episode.

References

Africa Intelligence (2005) 'The cash just keeps coming', 403(26)

Africa–Asia Confidential (2009) 'Luanda diversifies its portfolio', 2(11) http://www.africa-asia-confidential.com/article-preview/id/289/Luanda_diversifies_its_portfolio, accessed 5 April 2012.

Agência Lusa (2005) 'Refinaria do Lobito pode estar operacional em 2010' [Lobito Refinery could be operational in 2010], 5 December, http://www.angonoticias.com/Artigos/item/7347, accessed 10 April 2012

Agência Lusa – Shanghai office (2006) 'Petrolífera chinesa obtém áreas de exploração em Angola' [Chinese petroleum company obtains exploration areas in Angola], 13 June, http://noticias.uol.com.br/economia/ultnot/lusa/2006/06/13/ult3679u78.jhtm, accessed 10 April 2012.

Angop (2005a) 'Autorizada cessão de Contrato de Partilha de Produção do Bloco 18' [Authorised transfer of the production sharing contract for Block 18], 27 March, http://www.portalangop.co.ao/motix/pt_pt/noticias/economia/2005/2/12/Autorizada-cessao-Contrato-Partilha-Producao-Bloco,53e79a19-99cc-4d7e-ad20-73b4aed3b19e.html, accessed 1 April 2012.

Angop (2005b) 'Angola e China assinam nove acordos de cooperação' [Angola and China sign nine cooperation agreements], 25 February, http://www.portalangop.co.ao/motix/pt_pt/noticias/politica/2005/1/8/Angola-China-assinam-nove-acordos-cooperacao,952208c2-adec-4a88-960c-1ebf143e6ea8.html, accessed 5 April 2012.

Energy Compass (2009), 'Angola: China's complex connections', 14 August, http://www.energyintel.com/documentdetail.asp?document_id=633690, accessed 1 April 2012

Faucon, B. (2009) 'Sonangol wants to block Marathon's share to China', Dow Jones Newswires, 11 September, http://online.wsj.com/article/BT-CO-20090911-713371.html, accessed 5 December 2010.

Faucon, B. and Ordonez, I. (2011) 'Update: Angola awards oil rights in new frontier area', Dow Jones Newswires, 24 January, http://www.advfn.com/news_UPDATE-Angola-Awards-Oil-Rights-In-New-Frontier-Area_46147521.html, accessed 26 January 2011.

Levkowitz, L., Ross, M.M. and Warner, J.R. (2009) 'The 88 Queensway Group: a case study in Chinese investors' operations in Angola and beyond', Washington, US–China Economic and Security Review Commission, http://www.uscc.gov/The_88_Queensway_Group.pdf, accessed 12 April 2012

6 TAMING THE DRAGON: CHINA'S OIL INTERESTS IN ANGOLA

Marathon (2009) 'Marathon announces $1.3 billion sale of 20 percent interest in Angola block 32', press release, 1 July, http://www.marathon.com/News/Press_Releases/Press_Release/?id=1308708, accessed 8 February 2011.

Ministry of Finance of Angola (2010) 'Exportações e receitas de petróleo 2010: receitas consolidadas' [Petroleum exports and revenue 2010: consolidated income], http://www.minfin.gv.ao/docs/dspPetrolDiamond.htm, accessed 7 March 2011.

Ministry of Petroleum, department of planning and statistics (2010) 'Relatório de Actividades do Sector Petrolífero relativo ao ano 2009' [Report on the activities of the petroleum sector for the year 2009], Luanda, August

Neto, S. (2007) 'Sonangol incompatibiliza-se com Chineses e Franceses' [Sonangol becomes incompatible with the Chinese and French], Angonoticias, 3 March, http://www.angonoticias.com/Artigos/item/12632, accessed 5 April 2012.

Reed, S. (2006) 'A bidding frenzy for Angola's oil', 7 June, http://www.businessweek.com/globalbiz/content/jun2006/gb20060607_581473.htm, accessed 1 April 2012.

Scandinavian Oil and Gas (2010) 'Sinopec to acquire a stake in block 18, Angola', 2 April, http://www.scandoil.com/moxie-bm2/news/sinopec-to-acquire-a-stake-in-block-18-angola.shtml, accessed 5 December 2010.

Semanário Angolense [Angola Weekly] (2004), 'A Índia não está a dormir' [India is not sleeping], no.89

Sonangol Universo (2010) 'Sonangol 35 year milestone of success beckons', December.

Sunita (2010) 'Block 18, east zone, Angola, commercial asset valuation and forecast to 2027', 7 September, http://business.ezinemark.com/block-18-east-zone-angola-commercial-asset-valuation-and-forecast-to-2027-167100ffc6c.html, accessed 5 December 2010.

Trade and Finance Magazine (2007) 'Extending Chinese interests', 1 March, http://www.tradefinancemagazine.com/Article/2139295/Regions/23000/Extending-Chinese-interests.html, accessed 1 April 2012.

Upstream (2010) 'Marathon wraps up block 32 sale', 9 February, http://www.upstreamonline.com/live/article205997.ece, accessed 5 December 2010.

Vines, A., Wong, L., Weimer, M. and Campos, I. (2009) Thirst for African Oil: Asian National Oil Companies in Nigeria and Angola, London, Chatham House

7

One million houses? Chinese engagement in Angola's national reconstruction

Sylvia Croese

Introduction

Among the many challenges faced by the Angolan government in the reconstruction of the country since the end of the civil war in 2002 is the lack of decent housing for the majority of the rapidly growing Angolan population, particularly in the country's urban centres. In Angola, all land belongs to the state but during the war little was undertaken in terms of urban planning and development, formal land allocation and registration or infrastructure and housing maintenance.

While a number of relatively small-scale housing projects were initiated by the state in the first post-war years, it was not until the elections of 2008 that housing started to feature prominently on the government's reconstruction agenda, illustrated by a pledge to build one million houses in all the country's provinces by 2012. However, so far efforts to address the housing crisis through this national urbanism and housing programme have remained ad hoc, costly, centrally planned and implemented in line with the modernist model of development pursued by the MPLA (Movimento Popular de Libertação de Angola) government. This model has a strong focus on infrastructure and has been financed to a large extent through Chinese oil-backed loans.

This chapter critically analyses the implementation of Angola's housing policy in the post-war era, as a product of this model of development. While the government seeks to portray a picture of change, over the years this model has only become more entrenched as MPLA consolidates its power and partnership with China. The chapter concludes by identifying the limitations of this kind of approach to reconstruction and the challenges on the way to fulfilling the right to housing, let alone providing one million houses, for the Angolan people.

Towards national reconstruction

When Angola's war finally came to an end in 2002, international concern was mounting about the lack of transparency with regard to the management of the increasing oil revenues of the country and prospects for development (Global Witness 1999, 2002; Human Rights Watch 2001; IMF 2002). According to the IMF, Angola's financial situation was 'very weak' as a result of weak monitoring of oil revenue flows and the absence of public expenditure management controls. On average, between 1998 and 2002, 36 per cent of government expenditure was off budget and 11 per cent could not be accounted for at all and probably disappeared into what is referred to as the 'Bermuda Triangle' between the state oil company Sonangol, the treasury and the National Bank (Hodges 2004). Moreover, although real GDP growth was on the rise as a result of an oil boom, poverty was rife and the IMF considered Angola to face 'a serious humanitarian crisis' (IMF 2003).

Indeed, the Angolan government faced a gigantic challenge to rebuild the country. In 2003, it ranked at the bottom of the UNDP Human Development Index, taking 164th place out of 175 countries (UNDP 2004). Decades of war had resulted in millions of internally displaced people, large mined areas and the destruction and degradation of most of the country's physical, economic and social infrastructure and services.

Conditions were particularly critical in the cities, especially the capital Luanda, to which many people fled during the war looking for safety and economic survival. Most of the formal housing stock in the city dates from colonial times, which until independence was reserved for the Portuguese while the indigenous population was forced to build informally outside the city centre (Jenkins et al 2002). After independence, most of this stock was occupied illegally and later confiscated and rented out or sold by the Angolan state through the state secretariat for housing for symbolic prices. Virtually no formal housing construction took place during the war, apart from some state-led residential construction in Luanda and the provinces of Benguela and Kwanza Sul (Sita José 2005). Little was undertaken in terms of actual urban planning and development, formal land allocation and registration or infrastructure and housing maintenance. As a result, land and houses were acquired or built through informal mechanisms. Once built for about 500,000 people, by the end of the war Luanda had an estimated four million inhabitants.

Chinese engagement

Between 2004 and 2008, Angola experienced double digit GDP growth as a result of increased oil production combined with high oil prices on the international market. In the same period, loans for public project investments with a total value of over $15 billion were reportedly extended to the country, the largest being oil-backed (World Bank 2007: 50–1). This gave rise to the introduction of the term 'Angola mode', designating loans for infrastructure development whereby the repayment is made in terms of natural resources (Foster et al 2008: x). China was a key factor in the establishment of this model by being the first to offer Angola large loans under very favourable terms in order to finance and execute infrastructure projects, while Western countries were tying financing for reconstruction to improved transparency in the management of the country's oil revenues, poverty reduction strategies and IMF-monitored economic and financial reforms (Pacheco 2006).[1]

Diplomatic relations between China and Angola's MPLA government had been established in 1983 in a context of subsiding tensions in China's relationship with the Soviet Union and renewed attention to Black Africa (Jackson 1995: 417–20). In 2010, according to China's ambassador to Angola, Zhang Bolun, more than fifty state-owned companies and 400 private companies were involved in Angola's reconstruction, with 60,000 to 70,000 Chinese residing in the country (Angonoticias 2010, *Jornal de Angola* 2011a). This is a remarkable development and illustrative of China's rapid inroad on the African continent as part of its 'going out' policy.

In 2002, China Construction Bank and Export-Import (Exim) Bank funded a number of projects in Angola with a value of over $150 million. In 2004, the countries agreed on a $2 billion credit line negotiated under a 'Strategic Public-Private Partnership Framework Agreement' (Resolution 31/04 of 15 November). This credit line came to constitute the main source of funding for Angola's public investment programme for the period 2004–06, financing over 100 contracts in the areas of health, education, energy and water, agriculture, transport, social communication and public works. In 2007, two additional Exim Bank loan agreements were signed: one for $500 million to finance complementary works resulting from the first credit line and a second for another $2 billion to be spent on integrated infrastructure, roads and transportation (Campos and Vines 2008: 5–7; see also Alves 2010: 11–12).

Another important source of funding had become available in 2005 from a private entity called the China International Fund (CIF). This institution is part of a larger holding, Beiya International Development, also referred to as the '88 Queensway Group', the Hong Kong address of over thirty companies linked to the group (Levkowitz et al 2009). According to its website, its mission is to 'aim at South–South cooperation' and in this context it has provided at least $2.9 billion to an estimated $9.8 billion to Angola for infrastructure reconstruction (World Bank 2007: 50). Contrary to the Exim Bank loans, which are managed by the ministry of finance and a multisectoral technical office,[2] the CIF funds are managed by a separate entity, the GRN (Gabinete de Reconstrução Nacional). This organ was set up in 2004 in order to create a mechanism that was 'able to systematically and permanently accompany the most fundamental national reconstruction projects' (Decree Law 06/04 of 22 October). It is only accountable to the Angolan president, José Eduardo dos Santos, and run by his military advisor General Hélder Vieira Dias, alias 'Kopelipa'.

While rumours about the alleged mismanagement of Exim Bank loans led to the publication of data on the website of the Angolan ministry of finance with regard to the execution of projects, the use of GRN-managed funds remained highly untransparent. A government resolution of 2006 which lists national reconstruction projects to be funded by the CIF even classified these projects as confidential under the country's state secrets law.

This list (see table 7.1) contains twelve infrastructural projects as well as five technical studies and includes projects such as the rehabilitation of three railway lines and the construction of a new international airport and a new satellite city of Luanda, as well as 215,000 houses all over the country.

However, the disbursement of funds and hence the execution of most of the projects was either delayed or never materialised. In 2007, the ministry of finance had to step in and raise funding to ensure the continuation of projects, such as railway rehabilitation, by issuing $3.5 billion in treasury bonds (Campos and Vines 2008: 10; Alves 2010: 13). Other projects, such as infrastructure upgrading in the Cazenga municipality in Luanda, were relaunched in later years often involving Chinese but also Brazilian and Portuguese credit lines.[3]

Indeed, in January 2008 it was reported that the Angolan government had reduced its estimates of the funds provided through the CIF credit line by two-thirds (*Financial Times* 2008). This has led some to argue that 'if there was any truth in the figures published by the World Bank [i.e. the estimated $9.8 billion], cuts took place either because CIF was unable to raise the capital it had promised, even before the government announced the reductions, or because a large part of the GRN expenditure was off-budget' (Vines et al 2009: 53). In any case, and as we shall see further on, for the Chinese government the CIF fiasco, coupled with the effects of the global economic and financial crisis, signified an opportunity to strengthen its role as a fundamental partner and financier of Angola's reconstruction.[4]

Putting housing on the agenda

While new laws were passed in 2004 on urban and territorial planning (law 3/04 of 25 June), land (law 9/04 of 9 November) and the creation of a national institute for housing (decree 12/04 of 9 March), until 2006 the Angolan government did not have a policy on housing as such. Efforts to tackle the housing crisis were limited to a number of ad hoc, costly, centrally planned and implemented but relatively small-scale projects. Examples include the Aldeia Nova (new village) project in Kwanza Sul province, aimed at reintegrating war veterans in agro-industrial kibbutz-like villages, the Nova Vida (new life) project in Luanda, largely directed at civil servants, and the Zango project, meant to accommodate people evicted from areas in the capital now earmarked for development.[5] Despite these projects, state intervention in housing was marked more by large-scale demolitions of houses of the urban poor than their construction. Between 2001 and 2006, thousands of families were affected by evictions in Luanda, which were often carried out using intimidation and violence, excessive force, insufficient notice and inadequate compensation, while failing to offer opportunities for information and consultation (Amnesty International 2003, 2007; Human Rights Watch 2007).

Many others moved to the periphery of the city of their own accord, no longer able to afford the centre of the city, or renting out their houses there to foreign companies and their workers. These had started to flood the country as result of the oil and reconstruction boom, increasing the housing shortage and making prices skyrocket as the lack of local capacity to produce, import or transport raw materials made construction costs extremely high. This gave rise to a highly lucrative and unregulated rental, real estate and land market, making Luanda the most expensive city for expatriates in the world (Mercer 2010).[6]

While guaranteeing the universal right to housing (resolution 60/06 of 4 September), the housing laws that were eventually adopted essentially legalised the government's established housing practice, namely to 'discipline the unorganised expansion of cities and villages' while promoting 'new and dignified spaces for urban housing in accordance with the rules for territorial planning' (law 3/07 of 3 September).

However, as the CIF funding was not coming through, other sources of credit to build housing had to be found. This led to the signature of a memorandum of understanding in June 2007 by the head of GRN, General Kopelipa, and the president of CITIC Group, a Chinese state-owned company, for the construction of a new satellite town aimed at accommodating 200,000 people in Luanda's Kilamba Kiaxi municipality, 20km south-east of the city centre. Valued at $3.5 billion, the project was reported to be the largest of its kind China has ever contracted abroad.[7] To this effect, state reserves were identified for the construction of a total of three new cities within the capital metropolitan region, Dande,

Table 7.1 Contracts signed between the government of the Republic of Angola and companies of the People's Republic of China, in the sphere of national reconstruction

Projects	Specification
Rehabilitation of the City of Luanda	Rehabilitation works in the City of Luanda in five municipalities: Kilamba Kiaxi, Rangel, Ingombota, Cazenga and Sambizanga
Improvement of the infrastructure of Cazenga-Cariango	Construction of main drainage channels and pipes and infrastructure works in the municipalities of Cazenga-Cariango and related works
Construction of a drainage system and improvement of infrastructure in Precol and Suroca	Construction of main system for the improvement of infrastructure in Suroca and Precol and related works
Construction of drainage system (central) and diversions and improvement works at the Rua Senado da Câmara, Rio Seco and Maianga	Construction of the main pipeline system and infrastructure works at the Rua Senado da Câmara, Rio Seco and Maianga
Project of piped water distribution and supply	Renovation of 300km of water pipes, 300 stand-points, 2800 valves, 30,000 water meters, 13 pumps and 5 control stations
Construction of 215,000 residences in 24 cities of 18 provinces	Construction of 215,000 housing units with a total construction area of 31,436,709 m²
Rehabilitation of the road Luanda–Sumbe–Lobito	Rehabilitation works on a length of 497km including the reconstruction of the roads, bridges and ditches

Rehabilitation of the roads Malanje–Saurimo and Luena–Dundo	Rehabilitation works on a total length of 1,107km including the reconstruction of the roads, bridges and ditches
Rehabilitation of the Luanda railway line	Rehabilitation works on a length of 444km, including the reconstruction of roads, bridges, ditches and related installations
General rehabilitation of the Benguela railway line	Rehabilitation works on a length of 1,547km, including the reconstruction of roads, bridges, ditches and related installations
General rehabilitation of the Moçâmedes railway line	Rehabilitation works on a length of 1,003km, including the reconstruction of roads, bridges, ditches and related installations
New international airport for Luanda	EPC contract, preparation, supply and construction of a new airport including carport, cargo areas and related buildings
Studies and technical projects:	
Project for the construction of houses	Project for the construction of 215,000 housing units in a total construction area of 31,436,709m²
Infrastructure improvement works	Project for improvement works on five public infrastructures
General and urban planning for the new city of Luanda	General planning for a new city including proposals for urban management and development and planning
General and urban planning for the administrative centre of Luanda	General planning for the administrative centre including ministerial buildings, Supreme Court, Parliament, House of the President, etc.
Landscape project for Luanda	Landscape project for the administrative centre of Luanda

Source: Resolution 61/06 of 4 September, author's translation

Cacuaco and Luanda, as well as an area for state-led self-help building in Capari (decrees 62–65/07 of 13 August).

The following year, the government announced an even more ambitious plan: the construction of one million houses throughout the country by 2012, pledging 'to build new homes and real estate projects in order to achieve the one million houses goal, through state initiatives and public-private partnerships' (Government of the Republic of Angola 2008: 73). After MPLA won the elections in September 2008 with an 82 per cent majority, the president publicly reiterated the government's plan on World Habitat day which was held in Luanda in October 2008. In his speech, he announced the allocation of $50 billion for the fulfilment of the national housing programme based on a calculation of $50,000 per house (Portalangop 2008). Again, state reserves were identified covering 100,000 hectares in nearly all provinces of the country, some to be used by the respective provincial governments and some by GRN (decrees 80–112/08 of 26 September).

The birth of the Third Republic

Things seemed to be moving very fast, but the election victory and lingering effect of the oil boom may have given the president a false sense of prosperity. After approving the national urbanism and housing programme for the period 2009–12 (resolution 20/09 of 11 March) and organising a national conference on housing in April in Luanda, which affirmed the state's role as 'a guide, organiser and regulator of the national urbanism and housing programme' (resolution 77/09 of 7 September), it turned out that of the million houses, 685,000 would in fact have to be constructed through 'self-help building' (*auto-construção*). To this effect, 420,000 serviced plots were to be provided in urban areas and 265,000 plots in rural areas. Only 115,000 houses would be constructed by the government, while 120,000 would have to be constructed by the private sector and 80,000 through cooperatives.

It is very probable that this reformulation was the result of the global economic and financial crisis that had started to hit the country in 2008 through sharply declining oil prices. By the beginning of 2009, the impact of the lower prices hit the treasury with full force, leaving the government suddenly scrambling for money. Indeed, upon approval of the housing programme it did not even have a provisional budget in place, let alone the $50 billion promised by the president.[8] Hence, the year 2009 was marked by an active search for new sources of funding, with the government even reaching out to the IMF resulting in a $1.4 billion stand-by agreement to restore macroeconomic balances and rebuild international reserves (IMF 2009).

Meanwhile, despite the lack of a defined budget, a myriad of high-level working groups and commissions were installed by the president to work on the implementation of the housing programme. These included a working group to elaborate an executive housing programme (dispatch 27/08 of 4 November); a national commission for the implementation of the housing programme, as well as provincial commissions (dispatch 9/09 of 31 March); a technical central coordination group of the national commission for the technical and administrative execution of the housing programme (dispatch 9/09 of 31 March); and a technical group for the financial execution of the housing programme (dispatch 9/09 of 31 March).[9]

However, in the absence of results, a year later the president moved to take matters into his own hands by taking over the leadership of the national commission (presidential dispatch 22/10 of 12 May). He also downsized the commission to include only two ministers of state (civil and military bureaux), and the ministers of finance, of urbanism and construction and of administration of the territory. During its next meeting in August 2010, the president stated that the national commission was now ready to 'close the chapter of studies, discussion and approval of the housing programme and move on to the execution and monitoring phase' (Portalangop 2010).

This move signalled the birth of a 'Third Republic' that had come into being after the adoption of a new constitution in February 2010. In his end-of-year speech of 2009, the president had already announced the beginning of this new era to allow 'the tackling of problems that hadn't been handled before in the context of earlier phases of peace consolidation and national reconciliation and reconstruction' (Portalangop 2009). While progressive on the one hand, enshrining modern liberties and rights such as the right to housing and quality of life (article 85), the constitution also strengthened the position of the president.[10] This enabled him to proceed to establish the workings of this new order throughout 2010, shuffling and reshuffling people as well as government entities while increasingly centralising power and decision making.

The effects of the economic and financial crisis contributed to creating a sense of emergency in need of direct top-down intervention. When in July 2010 it became clear that the government had accumulated arrears worth $6.8 billion to companies that had executed projects of public investment, a number of new laws on budget execution and procurement were announced in order to put an end to 'irregular practices exercised by government institutions as well as companies' (Government of the Republic of Angola 2010 and *Jornal de Angola* 2010a). In a similar vein, government reshuffles were presented as the beginning of 'a new era of more responsible and transparent management of the public good, in order to promote the emergence of a firmer attitude in the combat against indiscipline and disorder' (*Jornal de Angola* 2010b).

By the end of the year, the president had disbanded the ministry of state for economic coordination, which had only come into being after the elections in 2008 as the ministry of economy. As a consequence its minister had to step down as minister of state, with the civil and military bureaux remaining at the core of executive power. Furthermore, Sonangol arose as a replacement of GRN in the area of housing as the management and commercialisation of the housing projects run by GRN were announced to be transferred to Sonangol Imobiliária (Sonip), a subsidiary of the state oil company that manages its real estate.[11] Similarly, the minister of urbanism and construction (formerly the ministry of public works, now merged with the ministry of urbanism and housing) was substituted by a former director of the Sonangol subsidiary Sonangol Integrated Logistic Services (Sonils) while a new governor was appointed for Luanda.[12]

One million houses?

What effect did the Third Republic's political configuration have on the implementation of the one million houses programme? To what extent were practices reflective of a new era and attitude introduced? In spite of the transparency discourse of the Third Republic, concrete information on the actual progress made on the objectives of the national urbanism and housing programme is not made available to the public. Thus, during the presentation of the 'balance' of the executive's activities in the last trimester of 2010 by the head of the civil bureau, Carlos Feijó, a practice instated after the adoption of the new constitution, little was said about how much progress had been made so far. Instead, new targets were announced for 2011 and 2012 (table 7.2) (*Jornal de Angola* 2011c: 3).

In these new, and rather confusing figures, cooperatives have been replaced by the private sector in general while what was formerly referred to as the private sector now seems to have passed to Sonangol. Mention is no longer made of the provision of rural land for self-help building, while the fact that the same figure for urban plots applies suggests that no plots have been delivered in the first half of the programme's timeline. Indeed, apart from some occasional references in the press during field visits to housing projects by the president, no information is available on how many and how plots of land have been allocated and equipped or provided with basic infrastructure and construction material for the purpose of self-help building.

A lot of work then seems to lie ahead. However, a new 'executive programme for the good governance of Luanda', promulgated by the civil bureau, only refers to the creation of technical community brigades and the use of government-provided construction kits for the execution of the self-help building programme in the capital. The section on land use and occupation in the programme includes a long list of administrative and legislative changes to be made with the main objective of criminalising illegal land occupation. To this particular effect, it states that the penal code should be changed to incorporate this as a public crime, municipal administrations should be strengthened to control illegal occupations in the periphery of the city with help of the military and the police, while those caught should be tried publicly in order to create examples for future prevention, all of this in order to 'strengthen the state's authority with regard to this illegal activity'. Institutional strengthening is to be achieved through 'administrative modernisation' and the creation of municipal 'technical units' (*Jornal de Angola* 2010d).

When faced with so much disorder and incapability, it does indeed seem much easier to focus on concrete projects that can

Table 7.2 Targets: National urbanism and housing programme 2009–12

	2009	2011
Self-help building	685,000 (420,000 urban and 265,000 rural)	420,000 (urban, of which 10,000 plots to be delivered by Sonangol)
Private sector (2009) Sonangol (2011)	120,000	120,000
Government	115,000	56 new urban areas with 144,037 social dwellings (including 10,000 self-built dwellings)
Cooperatives (2009) Private sector (2011)	80,000	80,000
Total	1,000,000	644,037

Source: Angolan press

be contracted out, signed into being with the simple stroke of a pen, using the product as bargaining chips in a next round of elections (scheduled for September 2012). This line of thinking, both the root as well as fruit of the political and institutional set-up of the Third Republic, and an increase in available financial resources may well have given rise to a new surge in social housing, upgrading and urban development project announcements.

Contracts for additional Chinese funds to finance urban development had been lined up since 2008 with the signing of a framework agreement for the extension of a $1.5 billion credit line by the China Development Bank (CDB) and negotiations over a $2.5 billion credit line to be conceded by the Industrial and Commercial Bank of China (ICBC) (Angop 2008, *Asian Banker* 2010). In November 2010, the president laid the first stone for the upgrading of the municipality of Cazenga (which had already been projected in 2006 in the list of confidential CIF-financed projects, see table 7.1) in order to transform the densely populated municipality from a 'suburban to an urban area with dignified services and houses', including the construction of 20,000 houses in the first phase of the project (*Jornal de Angola* 2010e). According to the

Chinese ambassador in an interview with *Jornal de Angola*, financing for the upgrading of both Cazenga and Sambizanga municipality is secured by the CDB loan, while the ICBC loan will be used for the construction of 100,000 houses in various provinces of the country (*Jornal de Angola* 2011a).

Recently, CITIC's work on the construction of the $3.5 billion-valued new town of Kilamba has been extended to include overall city planning with the signing of a contract for the elaboration of a strategic plan for the urban development of Luanda and an inter-municipal master plan for the municipalities of Belas and Kilamba Kiaxi. The project will reportedly cost $10.6 million and serve to 'organise the proper use of land in Luanda' (*Jornal de Angola* 2011d). The construction of thousands of houses in 'new centralities' in the state reserves of Dande (including Capari) and Cacuaco, as well as in the municipality of Viana, is already well underway, all involving Chinese contractors (Portalangop 2011a and 2011b).

Sonangol's real estate arm Sonip, which now oversees the construction of these new centralities in Luanda as well as in the rest of the country (construction is already in progress in the oil- and diamond-rich provinces, respectively, of Cabinda and Lunda Norte), has also partnered with the Israeli company LR Group (the company involved in the Aldeia Nova project in Kwanza Sul mentioned earlier) to form a company named Kora Angola, in a bid to build 40,000 houses by 2012 (Revista Exame Angola 2011). To finance the construction of these houses, use will be made of a previously extended oil-backed credit line of $750 million by LR Group, to be increased to $1.5 billion. Together with the reportedly 70,000 houses of the new centralities, this would contribute to meeting the government's stipulated delivery target for Sonangol of 120,000 houses.

Conclusion

Average urban growth in Luanda is projected to be higher (5.79 per cent) than in any other southern African city for the years 2005 to 2010 (UN-Habitat 2008: 137). Currently, the city accommodates an estimated six million (one third of the total population) of which two thirds live in informal settlements in the periphery and 60 per cent on less than $2 a day (DW and CEHS 2005, UCAN

2010). According to a nationwide government survey for 2008–09, as much as 90.9 per cent of the Angolan urban population lives in 'inappropriate conditions' (INE 2010).

The adoption of plans such as the national urbanism and housing programme are an indication of the government's awareness of the need to tackle problems in the area of housing and urban development. However, the approach practised so far is flawed.

Although the housing programme's main component, self-help housing, presents a cost-effective and participatory way of providing housing, as well as opportunities for local industries, all the government's efforts and resources are focused on state-built housing through external financial as well as material inputs.

While public housing might meet a need in terms of formal deficits, it is not clear whether the houses built meet people's practical needs as they were not consulted beforehand. There are many examples to be found elsewhere in the world where public housing has resulted in slummification (UN-Habitat 2003). This point does not even take into account the quality of Chinese construction, which is publicly questioned in Angola and generally regarded to be the result of deficient supervision.

The lack of supervision ties into another issue of concern, which is the legal gap in which the government's efforts are taking place. For instance, despite the fact that thousands of 'social houses' are being built, legislation which defines and regulates access to social housing is yet to be passed. Hence, the price of the first 3,000 apartments in the new town of Kilamba that were put on sale in 2011 ranged between $125,000 and $200,000 exceeding by far the $60,000 established by the Angolan president as the maximum price for a social house.[13] Moreover, because the majority of the projects are being financed through external credit lines, public scrutiny of how these funds are spent is limited.

In sum, by premising its policies on the aim of bringing order to disorder through centrally planned and executed housing projects, the Angolan government fails to take into account what people's real needs and capacities are. This jeopardises the sustainability of projects resulting from such policies, while structural problems related to the provision of basic services such as water and electricity, as well as to the management of the allocation, transfer and registration of land and access to credit for housing persist.

Thus, as elections are approaching again it seems that despite the Third Republic discourse on transparency and rigour, the government is sticking to a model for development which provides the seemingly safest, fastest and easiest but also most unaccountable way to meet targets that may only serve the interests of those already in power.

This chapter draws on the study, 'One million houses? Angola's national reconstruction and Chinese and Brazilian engagement', conducted with financial support of Fahamu's Emerging Powers in Africa Initiative, available at http://www.fahamu.org/images/ empowers_report_0311.pdf, accessed 3 March 2012.

Notes

1. Angola does have a poverty reduction strategy, which was elaborated by the ministry of planning and adopted by the council of ministers in 2003, but there was little ownership of this plan by the Angolan government as it was largely a result of external pressure. However, the majority of the indicators that were part of the plan can be found in the government's bi-annual programmes.
2. GAT, initially called the Gabinete de Apoio Técnico de Gestão da Linha de Crédito da China, provides technical support to the management of Chinese credit lines. Over time it came to function as the Gabinete de Apoio às Linhas de Crédito which includes the management of other credit lines than those from China.
3. See, for an overview of the different sources of financing for the development of Cazenga, the report in *Jornal de Angola* (2011b) and *O País* (2011).
4. A point also made by Alves (2010: 13).
5. To this effect a 'relocation department' (decree 57/01 of 21 September) had been created in 2001, managed by an office that had been set up in 1998 to implement and oversee special works, better known as the GOE (Gabinete de Obras Especiais).
6. To date, the rental and real estate market continues unregulated by Angolan law, perhaps because for many it has provided a very lucrative source of income (e.g. houses acquired under government schemes after independence or bought on the private market could now be rented out or sold for many times the original price paid). At the time of writing, new legislation on urban rental and real estate mediation was circulating, but not yet approved.
7. See *People's Daily* (2008) and also www.cici.citic.com.
8. The resolution which approved the programme called for the ministries of economy and of finance to 'support the conclusion of a provisional

budget for the national urbanism and housing programme and a financing mechanism for the national urbanism and housing system' (resolution 20/09 of 11 March, art. 2).

9. It is quite mysterious why the ministry of economy, previously identified as responsible for concluding the provisional budget, does not feature in any of these commissions, signalling perhaps its imminent demise.

10. The new constitution instated a presidential parliamentary system, ruling out earlier announced presidential elections. To assist the president in exercising their executive power, positions were created for a vice president and three ministers of state: one for civil, one for military and one for economic affairs. The post of prime minister ceased to exist.

11. Other infrastructure projects involving roads, railways and the rehabilitation of social infrastructure were to be transferred to other relevant entities (*Jornal de Angola* 2010c). On the workings of Sonangol, refer to Soares de Oliveira (2007).

12. The new governor of Luanda, José Maria dos Santos, was sacked a little over eight months later.

13. The maximum price for a social house was announced by the president in the speech he made during the national housing commission meeting of August 2010. It had already gone up from the previously announced price of $50,000. See Marques de Morais (2011) for a critical analysis of the Kilamba project as a model of corruption.

References

Angonotícias (2010) 'Mais de 50 grandes empresas estatais chinesas envolvidas na reconstrução do país', 19 November, http://www.angonoticias.com/full_headlines.php?id=29415, accessed 20 November 2010

Angop (2008) 'Governo angolano e Banco de Desenvolvimento da China analisam cooperação', 23 September, http://www.portalangop.co.ao/motix/pt_pt/noticias/economia/Governo-angolano-Banco-Desenvolvimento-China-analisam-cooperacao,c3289365-36c6-47dd-b967-893f9ec4418e.html, accessed 13 March 2012

Alves, A.C. (2010) 'The oil factor in Sino-Angolan relations at the start of the 21st century', *Occasional Paper*, 55, Johannesburg, SAIIA, http://www.saiia.org.za/images/stories/pubs/occasional_papers/saia_sop_55_alves_20100225.pdf, accessed 13 March 2012

Amnesty International (2003) 'Angola: Mass forced evictions in Luanda. A call for a human rights based housing policy', AI Index: AFR 12/007/2003, 12 November, http://www.amnesty.org/en/library/asset/AFR12/007/2003/en/eccbe3e6-d691-11dd-ab95-a13b602c0642/afr120072003en.pdf, accessed 13 March 2012

Amnesty International (2007) 'Angola: Lives in ruins. Forced evictions continue', AI Index: AFR 12/001/2007, 15 January, http://www.amnesty.org/en/library/asset/AFR12/001/2007/en/5a0a5f09-d3c5-11dd-8743-d305bea2b2c7/afr120012007en.pdf, accessed 13 March 2012

Asian Banker (2010) 'Interview with Jiang Jianqing, chairman of Industrial and Commercial Bank of China, 16 March 2010, 25 March, http://www.prnewswire.com/news-releases/interview-industrial-and-commercial-bank-of-china-chairman-jiang-jianqing-89100627.html, accessed 13 March 2012

Campos, I. and Vines, A. (2008) 'Angola and China: a pragmatic partnership', Working paper presented at a CSIS conference 'Prospects for improving US–China–Africa relations', http://www.chathamhouse.org/sites/default/files/public/Research/Africa/angolachina_csis.pdf, accessed 17 April 2012

DW and CEHS (2005) 'Terra. Reforma sobre a terra urbana em Angola no período pós-guerra: pesquisa, advocacia e políticas de desenvolvimento', *Development Workshop Occasional Paper*, 6, Luanda, Development Workshop

Financial Times (2008) 'Infrastructure: big projects fall behind schedule', 23 January, http://www.ft.com/cms/s/0/58079b3a-c897-11dc-94a6-0000779fd2ac,dwp_uuid=8735dcb2-be8a-11dc-8c61-0000779fd2ac.html#axzz15LBO5WjY, accessed 13 March 2012.

Foster, V., Butterfield, W., Chen, C. and Pushak, N. (2008) 'Building bridges: China's growing role as infrastructure financier for sub-Saharan Africa', *Trends and Policy Options*, 5, World Bank and Public-Private Infrastructure Advisory Facility, http://siteresources.worldbank.org/INTAFRICA/Resources/Building_Bridges_Master_Version_wo-Embg_with_cover.pdf, accessed 13 March 2012

Global Witness (1999) *A Crude Awakening: The Role of the Oil and Banking Industries in Angola's Civil War and the Plunder of State Assets*, London, Global Witness

Global Witness (2002) *All The President's Men: The Devastating Story of Oil and Corruption in Angola's Privatised War*, London, Global Witness

Government of the Republic of Angola (2008) *Programa de Governo 2009–12*

Government of the Republic of Angola (2010) 'Memorando. Situação da regularização dos atrasados internos de 2008 e 2009 respeitantes ao programa de investimentos públicos e seu impacto económico', Luanda, ministry of finance, 2 July

Hodges, A. (2004) *Angola: Anatomy of an Oil State*, Oxford, James Currey

Human Rights Watch (2001) *The Oil Diagnostic in Angola: An Update*, New York and London, Human Rights Watch

Human Rights Watch (2007) *They Pushed Down the Houses: Forced Evictions and Insecure Land Tenure for Luanda's Urban Poor*, New York, Human Rights Watch

IMF (2002) *Angola: Staff Report for the 2002 Article IV Consultation*, International Monetary Fund, Washington DC, March

IMF (2003) *Angola: Staff report for the 2003 Article IV Consultation*, International Monetary Fund, Washington DC, July

IMF (2009) 'IMF Executive Board approves US$1.4 billion stand-by agreement', press release 09/425, 23 November, http://www.imf.org/external/np/sec/pr/2009/pr09425.htm, accessed 13 March 2012

INE (2001) *Inquérito de Indicadores Múltiplos 2001*, Luanda, Instituto Nacional de Estatística

INE (2010) *Inquérito Integrado Sobre o Bem-Estar da População 2008–09*, Luanda, Instituto Nacional de Estatística

Jackson, S. (1995) 'China's third world foreign policy: the case of Angola and Mozambique, 1961–93', *The China Quarterly*, 142: 388–422

Jenkins, P., Robson, P. and Cain, A. (2002) 'City profile. Luanda', *Environment and Urbanization*, 19(2): 139–50

Jornal de Angola (2010a) 'Ministério das finanças esclarece que dívidas estão a ser pagas', 20 July, http://jornaldeangola.sapo.ao/20/0/ministerio_das_financas_esclarece_que_dividas_estao_a_ser_pagas_1, accessed 13 March 2012

Jornal de Angola (2010b) 'Mudanças no executivo vão dar força à nova era', 30 November, http://jornaldeangola.sapo.ao/20/0/mudancas_no_executivo_vao_dar_forca_a_nova_era, accessed 13 March 2012

Jornal de Angola (2010c) 'Imobiliária da Sonangol gere novas centralidades', 28 September, http://jornaldeangola.sapo.ao/20/0/imobiliaria_da_sonangol_gere_novas_centralidades, accessed 13 March 2012

Jornal de Angola (2010d) 'Civismo e organização para recuperar Luanda', 4 December, http://jornaldeangola.sapo.ao/20/0/civismo_e_organizacao_para_recuperar_luanda, accessed 27 June 2011

Jornal de Angola (2010e) 'Presidente coloca primeira pedra para requalificação do Cazenga', 8 November, http://jornaldeangola.sapo.ao/20/0/presidente_coloca_primeira_pedra_para_requalificacao_do_cazenga, accessed 13 March 2012

Jornal de Angola (2011a) 'China quer aumentar áreas de cooperação', 21 March, http://jornaldeangola.sapo.ao/25/0/china_quer_aumentar_areas_de_cooperacao, accessed 3 March 2012

Jornal de Angola (2011b) 'Ministro do urbanismo e construção aponta acções de prioritária', 27 May, http://jornaldeangola.sapo.ao/20/0/ministro_do_urbanismo_e_construcao_aponta_accoes_de_execucao_prioritaria, accessed 3 March 2012

Jornal de Angola (2011c) 'Lei sobre segurança nacional em preparação. Executivo apresentou ontem o balanço do último trimestre do ano passado', 18 January

Jornal de Angola (2011d) 'Luanda tem plano para urbanização dos municípios', 27 May, http://jornaldeangola.sapo.ao/20/0/luanda_tem_plano_para_urbanizacao_dos_municipios, accessed 13 June 2011

Levkowitz, L., Ross, M.M. and Warner, J.R. (2009) 'The 88 Queensway Group: a case study in Chinese investors' operations in Angola and beyond', Washington, US–China Economic and Security Review Commission, http://www.uscc.gov/The_88_Queensway_Group.pdf, accessed 12 April 2012

Marques de Morais, R. (2011) 'The ill-gotten gains behind Angola's Kilamba housing development', *Pambazuka News*, 552, http://pambazuka.org/en/category/features/77070, accessed 3 March 2012

Mercer (2010) *Cost of Living Survey 2010*, www.mercer.com/costofliving, accessed 13 March 2012

O País (2011) 'Requalificação do Cazenga custa USD 800 milhões', 30 May, http://www.opais.net/pt/opais/?id=1929&det=21280, accessed 3 March 2012

Pacheco, F. (2006) 'The role of external development actors in post-conflict scenarios – the case of Angola', Centro de Estudos Sociais (Centre for Social Studies) No. 258, http://www.ces.uc.pt/publicacoes/oficina/258/258. pdf, accessed 13 March 2012

People's Daily (2008) 'Chinese company launches $3.5 bln housing project in Angola', 2 September, http://english.people.com. cn/90001/90776/90884/6491378.html, accessed 3 March 2012

Portalangop (2008) 'Discurso do presidente da república sobre o dia mundial do habitat', 6 October, http://www.portalangop.co.ao/motix/pt_pt/ noticias/politica/Discurso-Presidente-Republica-sobre-Dia-Mundial-Habitat,47e3edf1-8e53-404a-8b33-b6af48642922.html, accessed 13 March 2012

Portalangop (2009) 'Íntegra do discurso do Presidente José Eduardo dos Santos', 28 December, http://www.portalangop.co.ao/motix/pt_pt/ noticias/politica/2009/11/53/Integra-discurso-Presidente-Jose-Eduardo-dos-Santos,d8280b3f-0a30-4656-91c4-ec75aef3c3c5.html, accessed 13 March 2012

Portalangop (2010) 'Íntegra do discurso do presidente da república', 5 August, http://www.portalangop.co.ao/motix/pt_pt/noticias/ politica/2010/7/31/Integra-discurso-Presidente-Republica,a66e513f-fff5-4472-b6de-6af444d5e8e5.html, accessed 13 March 2012

Portalangop (2011a) 'Administrador de Cacuaco congratula-se com construção de nova cidade', 17 September, http://www.portalangop. co.ao/motix/pt_pt/noticias/politica/2011/8/37/Administrador-Cacuaco-congratula-com-construcao-nova-cidade,54f3a54b-162b-4335-84c0-4cc1c5cb9b9b.html, accessed 18 September 2011

Portalangop (2011b) 'Centralidade do Musseque Capari fica pronto em 2012', 6 December, http://www.portalangop.co.ao/motix/pt_pt/noticias/ sociedade/2011/11/49/Centralidade-Musseque-Capari-fica-pronta-2012,a0d157fe-c3bc-4582-8ee4-c87278b7b194.html, accessed 15 December 2011

Revista Exame Angola (2011) 'O nome de código é Kora', 16 March, http:// www.exameangola.com/pt/?id=1999&det=19742&ss=%91O%20nome%20 de%20c%F3digo%20%E9%20Kora%92, accessed 3 March 2012

Sita José, D. (2005) 'Políticas habitacionais: situação do quadro habitacional em Angola', in *A juventude face à reconstrução e ao desenvolvimento do país. Anais da IX Jornada Técnico-Científica*, Luanda, Fundação Eduardo dos Santos

Soares de Oliveira, R. (2007) 'Business success, Angola style: postcolonial politics and the rise and rise of Sonangol', *Journal of Modern African Studies*, 45(4): 595–619

UCAN (2010) *Relatório Económico de Angola 2009*, Luanda, Centro de Estudos e Investigação Ciêntífica (CEIC), Núcleo de Macroeconomia, Universidade Católica de Angola

UNDP (2004) *Human Development Report 2004. Cultural liberty in today's diverse world*, United Nations Development Programme

UN-Habitat (2003) *The Challenge of Slums: Global Report on Human Settlements 2003*, London, Earthscan Publications

UN-Habitat (2008) *The State of African Cities 2008. A Framework for Addressing Urban Challenges in Africa*, Nairobi, UN-Habitat

Vines, A., Wong, L., Weimer, M. and Campos, I. (2009) *Thirst for African Oil: Asian National Oil Companies in Nigeria and Angola*, London, Chatham House

World Bank (2007) 'International Development Association Interim Strategy Note for the Republic of Angola. Report No. 39394-AO', April 26, www-wds.worldbank.org/external/default/.../WDSP/.../39394main.pdf, accessed 13 March 2012

8

Chinese corporate practices in Angola – myths and facts

Amalia Quintão and Regina Santos

China in Africa

The new economic relations between China and Africa represent one of the recent but significant developments in the region. In fact, China is in the process of becoming not only the most important commercial partner for Africa but also of obtaining privileged positions in different sectors. China's economic presence is becoming increasingly strong in the continent with regard to the establishment of construction companies and involvement in infrastructure rehabilitation, petroleum and mines, as well as through loans and funding for very large-scale local projects.

This strong presence of Chinese multinationals in Africa is explained by the need to supply China with raw materials and energy for the development of its industries and at the same time the need to open new frontiers for its export market. Included in this expansion is the search for employment for an ever-increasing population with growing rates of unemployment.

The African continent has become increasingly interested in China, a fact which led to the creation of the China–Africa Cooperation Forum in 2000 and the Forum for Economic and Trade Cooperation between China and Portuguese-speaking Countries (which excludes São Tomé and Principe) in 2003. This forum, with the Community of Portuguese-speaking Countries, is an official mechanism for cooperation that is non-political in nature, the key to which is cooperation and economic development. The objective is to strengthen collaboration and economic exchanges between the People's Republic of China and the Portuguese-language countries, to dynamise the role of Macau as a platform to link these countries and to promote the development of links between China, Macau and the Portuguese-language countries.

China in Angola

China, with its strong financial capacity together with the performance of its companies, became the solution the Angolan government was looking for to confront the serious infrastructure-related problems resulting from the war, both from a reconstruction perspective and with regard to the development of new capacities.

For Angola today, China is an important partner enabling Angola to continue its national reconstruction at an accelerated pace, in spite of the current crisis being experienced worldwide.

China concretised the opportunity to finance the reconstruction of infrastructure destroyed by the war after Angola's disenchantment with the international community which, when Angola sought a donor's conference, made political demands that the government of Angola was not inclined to accept.

While Angola needs to develop its economy China needs natural resources. Angola desires a fruitful partnership, different from those it has experienced to date, safeguarding its right to choose between the largest number of partners.

Bilateral cooperation treaties

The dynamic of economic and trade relations between the two countries has configured a new framework for cooperation based on principles of equality, reciprocal advantages and joint development.

Bilateral relations have developed favourably and both countries wish to expand and consolidate their cooperation. Official visits at the highest level by various members of both governments have worked as an incentive towards an increase in cooperation treaties.

Many of the agreements aim at expanding economic ties, strengthening financial cooperation and learning from China about construction and development. China has managed to obtain a significant economic position in Angola, firstly as an oil importer, secondly as a major allocator of funds and thirdly as the primary developer of the main projects to rebuild the country's infrastructure.

Since the end of 2003, economic cooperation between Angola and China has expanded significantly as a result of China granting credit for the development of economic and social projects in various fields as part of the national reconstruction programme.

Table 8.1 shows the development of treaties broken down into two distinct periods, the first a 20-year period (1984–2003) with 14 signed agreements, and the second a 5-year period (2004–08) during which the number of agreements almost doubled.

According to the Angolan government, the advantage of cooperation with China compared with other countries lies in the fact that no political conditions are imposed with regard to credit volumes, funding conditions, work implementation deadlines, levels of productivity or the way in which the technicians are involved in the urban and rural environment.

China–Angola trade relations

Angola has the largest lines of credit from China of any African country and today holds first place with regard to commercial partnerships between Africa and China. China's extraordinary economic growth is only possible with the supply of raw materials, of which petroleum is the most important, and Angola was

Table 8.1 Development of bilateral cooperation treaties with China

Cooperation treaties	1984–2003	2004–2008
Cooperation agreements	6	12
Cooperation protocols	4	1
Memorandum of understanding	0	4
Treaties, contracts, memoranda	0	3
Other agreements	4	6
Total	14*	26**

* In the areas of finance, banking, culture, economics, technical, trade promotion, commissions
** Including finance, banking, culture, economics, technical, energy resources, health, justice, construction, education, commissions

Source: Ministry of foreign relations (2009)

its second largest supplier in 2010, accounting for 42.8 per cent of Angolan total oil exports (Banco Nacional de Angola 2011). Apart from being one of the main exporters of petroleum to China, Angola is also one of the countries in which the most Chinese construction companies are working. In turn Angola, with the opening up of its offshore access for the petroleum industry, is a country in which Chinese petroleum companies – Sinopec and China National Petroleum Corporation (CNPC) – can learn to deal with all matters related to exploration and production in deep water, together with the major Western petroleum companies currently active in Angola.

Around 90 per cent of Angola's imports from China are consumable goods and the remainder are capital goods, while Angolan exports are mainly petroleum (88 per cent), diamonds and scrap iron. In 2010, the bilateral trade volume reached $24.8 billion, a growth of 45.3 per cent compared with 2009 (*Novo Jornal* 2011).

The first funds from China arrived at a time when Angola was continually finding the doors of international financial institutions closed. Funding granted by China for projects related to national reconstruction and the relaunching of the Angolan economy reached $14.5 billion by the end of 2010, according to official sources (*Jornal de Angola* 2011).

Statistics from the National Private Investment Agency (ANIP) suggest that foreign direct investment (FDI) from China to Angola, not related to the petroleum sector, comes mainly from Chinese state companies and is worth approximately $70 million. Compared with other countries, there has been a significant growth in recent years in areas not related to hydrocarbons. Energy, infrastructure and finance are the three main sectors of cooperation.

Characteristics of Chinese companies

For several decades, China was isolated from the global economy and during this period there was internal development of large companies, mainly in the areas of mining, technology and construction. The strong presence of Chinese multinationals in Africa is explained by the need to supply China with raw materials and energy for the development of its industries as well as the need to open new frontiers for its export market.

Cooperation between China and Angola is a way for Chinese companies to enter into the market. Projects completed by Chinese companies in Angola are funded by lines of credit from Chinese banks. Agreements stipulate the recruitment of 30 per cent of national contractors but Chinese contractors are often not able to meet required standards; they say that national materials are more expensive, manpower is slower and it is difficult to meet the stipulated deadlines. On the other hand, Chinese companies have been criticised for their business model, their labour practices and their contribution towards local development.

Comparative economic advantages

China's financial and economic capacity ranks it among the largest national economies in the world and it is currently entering a new phase of its history, with the birth of its multinational companies. In the same way as China has created its own appropriate development model, it is creating its companies according to a business prototype that differentiates them from the Western multinational companies in the global market.

Local participation by companies and services limited to 30 per cent of the contracts funded by Chinese credit lines has thus raised concern with regard to the potential national benefit in terms of added value and employment generation.

Apprehensions regarding the Chinese presence Contracts are negotiated on a bilateral basis via a global package whereby China provides multibillion dollar concessional loans for infrastructure to be repaid in oil. As part of the deal Chinese companies are to undertake the projects employing their own workers and sourcing the content in China, which has significant implications on the economic, social and political level:

- Substitution of national manpower with Chinese manpower
- Substitution of Angolan contractors with Chinese companies in the main growth sectors of the economy, civil construction, telecommunications and energy
- Near-exclusive monopoly of Chinese companies in some sectors

- Dependence on the importation of materials and equipment of Chinese origin.

The stipulation in the agreements that only 30 per cent of contractors in projects need to be Angolan nationals means that Chinese workers are dominant in almost all of the main projects in Angola, from the construction of schools, basic sanitation networks (water and sewage), electrical energy, communication and urban infrastructure.

The large amount of unqualified manpower coming to Angola to work in Chinese companies naturally causes a reaction among Angolan workers. This also creates a disadvantage in relation to the Western companies who are obliged to contract Angolans, only using expatriates when they are able to prove that the market does not contain the specialisations they require, which takes some time. Chinese companies are completely exempt from this regulation.

Corporate social responsibility practices A series of studies suggest that the practices of multinational companies with regard to social responsibility and other similar areas depend on the country in which their activities are being developed (Ashley et al 2000).

Corporate social responsibility, where companies voluntarily incorporate environmental and social issues in their businesses and interaction with the government, clients, employees, investors, etc, extends their role beyond purely economic objectives. This concept has become increasingly topical and it is widely believed that a company's activities cannot be disassociated from the practice of citizenship actions.

Western companies are guided by the protection of certain ethical values but often, in practice, commercial interests are superimposed over everything else, as happens with Chinese companies. However, social responsibility practices in Angola are less evident in Chinese than in Western companies who, in general, operate with more transparency and social commitment, in most cases pressurised by civil society institutions and organisations from their respective countries.

Case study: Angolan workers' perception of the Chinese in Angola

The case study investigated the activities of Chinese companies in Angola, based on the perception of Angolan workers employed either in Chinese companies or Western companies, and of the effects of that activity on the economy.

The objective was to perceive the impact of China on the labour market in order to extract evidence of attitudes to corporate social responsibility related to safety, salary differences, working hours, working conditions and the transfer of technology and knowledge. In this way, the positioning of foreign companies in Angola, both Chinese and Western, could be seen, which would contribute towards defining employment policies.

This investigation was a statistical survey based on questionnaires. The intention was not to conduct a theoretical study but

Figure 8.1 Survey respondents' employment by sector

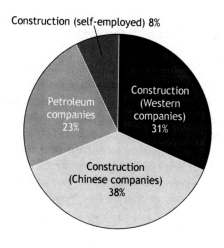

Source: Worker surveys by the authors, 2010

an evaluation of workers' perceptions of Chinese companies in Angola, through several closed and open questions such as:

With the arrival of Chinese companies:
- Did it become more difficult for Angolans to find work?
- Did working conditions worsen for Angolan workers?
- Did this lead to longer working hours for Angolan workers?

Compared with Angolans, are Chinese workers:
- Willing to work for lower salaries?
- Willing to work in worse working conditions?
- Better workers?
- Willing to work longer hours?

Do Chinese companies:
- Offer good and safe working conditions?
- Pay good salaries?

Do Angolan workers work well with the Chinese?

Can Angolan workers learn a lot from the Chinese?

Is it preferable to work for a Western company or a Chinese company, in a scenario where both are paying the same salaries?

Sample characterisation

The sample field, a total of 325 Angolan workers, grouped into construction companies (Western and Chinese),[1] self-employed (all in the civil construction sector) and petroleum companies, were distributed as in table 8.2.

The selection of companies to survey was mainly based on sectors with a high level of involvement by Chinese companies. Various difficulties were encountered in this study, from the selection of companies to the cooperation of persons to be surveyed.

Table 8.2 Survey respondents' employment by sector and company

Sector	Companies	%
Civil construction (Western)	Zagope	7.7
	Odebrecht	7.7
	Somague	7.7
	Soares Da Costa	7.7
	subtotal	30.8
Civil construction (Chinese)	Sinohydro	7.7
	China Jiangsu International	20.0
	GRN-CITIC Construction	10.8
	subtotal	38.5
Civil construction (self-employed)	self-employed	7.7
	Total (civil construction)	77
Petroleum	Service provision to petroleum companies	9.2
	Petroleum companies	13.8
	Total (petroleum)	23
	TOTAL	100

Source: Worker surveys by the authors, 2010

Results of the survey

Employment conditions in companies Important findings were extracted from the analysis of the survey results with regard to the social responsibility practices of Chinese corporations in Angola. The following should be highlighted:

- Approximately 40 per cent of workers in Chinese companies are under 22 years of age. This figure is 18 per cent in Western companies and 9 per cent in petroleum companies.

- 76 per cent of workers in Chinese companies have less than one year of work experience; this figure is only 34 per cent in Western companies.
- Approximately 84 per cent of those surveyed in Chinese companies work over 8 hours per day, compared to 73 per cent in Western companies.
- 80 per cent of workers in Chinese companies and 50 per cent in Western companies are only educated up to primary level.
- 86 per cent of workers in Chinese companies earn less than $300 per month, as opposed to Western companies where this percentage is 33 per cent.

It was confirmed that there is a high turnover of workers in Chinese companies, where the average employment time is short. This is due partly to the type of work and partly to the contracting system, as presented in figure 8.2.

Figure 8.2 Period of employment by sector

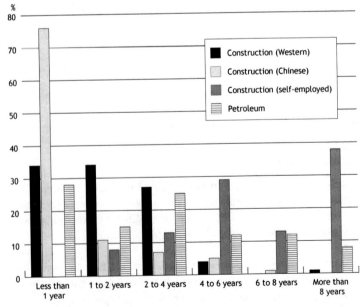

Source: Worker surveys by the authors, 2010

Figure 8.3 shows that according to the perception of workers, Angolans in Chinese companies work longer hours than Angolan workers in Western companies.

Chinese companies offer lower salaries, as shown by figure 8.4, and probably because of this, employment instability is greater.

Those working in Chinese companies tend to confirm (more than workers in other companies) that the Chinese are willing to work for lower salaries than Angolans. Chinese companies appear to violate labour standards more often, by allowing or encouraging working days exceeding eight hours. However, the results indicate that in reality, working-hour violations occur in most Western companies. Working-hour regulations are violated to a lesser extent in petroleum companies. It is possible that the reason for this is the nature of the work and the salary levels offered, as seen in figure 8.5.

Cultural, linguistic and historical differences were evident

Figure 8.3 Daily working hours by sector

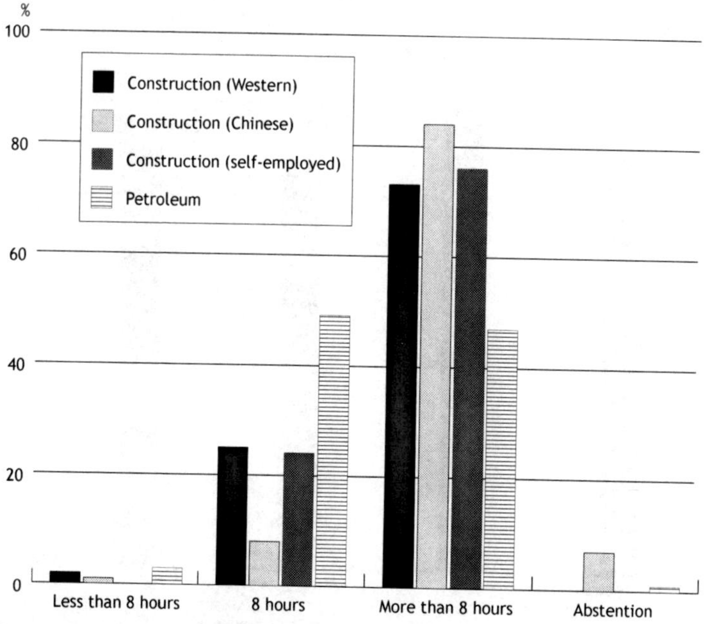

Source: Worker surveys by the authors, 2010

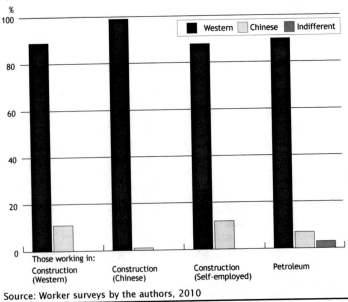

Figure 8.4 Monthly salary by sector

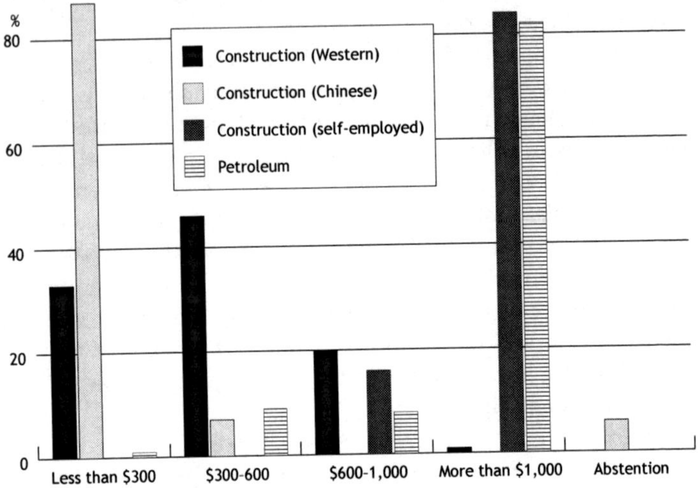

Source: Worker surveys by the authors, 2010

Figure 8.5 Preference for Chinese or Western companies by sector where both pay the same

Source: Worker surveys by the authors, 2010

with regard to workers' preferences for either Chinese or Western companies (for the same salary) and there are obvious incompatibilities between Chinese and Angolan workers.

These factors contribute towards explaining why the majority of Angolan workers would rather work for Western companies than Chinese companies, and why the majority would want a salary increase of between 20 and 60 percent for them to prefer to work for Chinese companies. Apart from a salary increase, many would want an employment contract (most Angolan workers in Chinese companies do not have one).

Perceptions of Chinese workers

In spite of the unfavourable comparison of Chinese companies with Western companies, Angolan workers in Chinese companies have a more favourable impression of Chinese workers than that held by Angolan workers in Western companies. We believe that the following results are very important in abolishing some myths that

Figure 8.6 Perception that Angolans and Chinese work well together, by sector

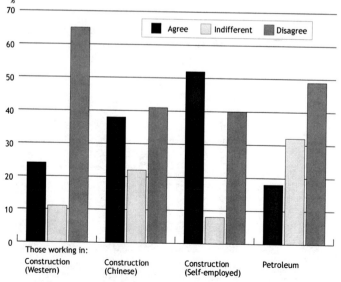

Source: Worker surveys by the authors, 2010

Figure 8.7 Perception that the Chinese work better than the Angolans, by sector

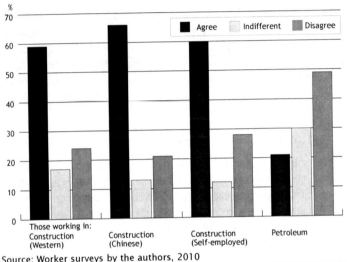

Source: Worker surveys by the authors, 2010

Figure 8.8 Perception that Angolans have a lot to learn from the Chinese

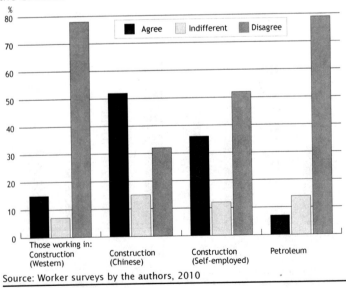

Source: Worker surveys by the authors, 2010

exist about the 'unknown' and indicate that as Angolan workers get used to the Chinese ways, this perception tends to normalise.

For example, we can conclude that Angolan workers with Chinese colleagues have a greater tendency to believe that Angolans and Chinese work well together, than those with no Chinese colleagues, as indicated in figure 8.6.

Those working with the Chinese tend to confirm the fairly universal impression that the Chinese work better than the Angolans, as shown in figure 8.7.

Also to emerge was the fact that more of those who know the Chinese than of those who do not work in Chinese companies believe that Angolans have a lot to learn from the Chinese, as seen in figure 8.8.

Conclusions and recommendations

In Angola, the Chinese strategy for granting loans, lines of credit and other support facilitates the entrance of Chinese companies. Like many other African countries, Angola must look for the best way of making use of the opportunities offered by a relationship with China, with the relevant economic policies and consolidation of national institutions, so as to maximise benefits in current and future relations.

On the one hand, there are obvious risks that the survey results tend to confirm. The arrival of Chinese workers is a significant social event in a continent with high levels of unemployment. The distortion of the labour market with low salaries and the low professional level of the workforce are impediments to development, increased productivity and family income. It appears that Chinese companies offer the worst working conditions. The fact that Chinese companies do not respect the clause to contract 30 per cent of services from the local market means that Chinese investment has had barely any impact on local employment creation.

On the other hand, there have been important positive messages. The perception held by Angolan workers with regard to the presence of Chinese companies is different in many aspects depending on the company in which the workers are employed. Apart from the novelty of the entrance of the Chinese, workers employed in Chinese companies and with Chinese colleagues are inclined to demystify the new partner. Their perceptions may be interpreted to confirm that Angolan workers are able to work well with the Chinese and learn new methods.

Taking these observations into account, it may be concluded that the Angolan government needs to create policies to guarantee working conditions in general, and in Chinese companies in particular.

We are convinced that cultural, economic and professional interchanges can be of significant benefit. The results appear to indicate that the demystification of relationships with Chinese partners may be advantageous: Angolan workers should seize the opportunity and the government should encourage this interchange. Evidently, we can assume that there is an interdependent relationship between working conditions and effective learning.

Notes

1. Western companies: Zagope, Odebrecht, Somague, Soares da Costa; Chinese companies: Sinohydro, China Jiangsu Internacional, GRN-CITIC Construction.
2. Petroleum companies were broken down into 60 per cent petroleum exploration companies and the rest, 40 per cent, service providers to petroleum companies

Bibliography

Aguilar, R. and Goldstein, A. (2009) 'The Chinization of Africa: the case of Angola', *The World Economy*, 32(11)

Alden, C. and Davies, M. (2006), 'A profile of the operations of Chinese multinationals in Africa', *South African Journal of International Affairs*, 13(1)

Alden, C. (2007) *China in Africa*, London, Zed Books

ANIP (2010) 'Guia do Investidor – proteccao ao investimento', http://www.anip.co.ao/Guia-do-Investidor/Proteccao-ao-Investimento.aspx, accessed 15 April 2012.

Ashley, P.A., Coutinho, R.B.G. and Tomei, P.A. (2000) 'A responsabilidade social corporativa e cidadania empresarial: uma análise conceitual comparativa" [Corporate social responsibility and corporate citizenship: a comparative conceptual analysis], *Revista do Terceiro Setor*, 2(99)

Banco Nacional de Angola (2011) 'Angola destino das exportacoes de Petroleo Bruto 2006–2010', http://www.bna.ao/uploads/{59b6189a-57b6-4cfb-add5-929fbe611a3c}.pdf, accessed 21 December 2011

Campos, I. and Vines, A. (2008) 'Angola and China: a pragmatic partnership', Working paper presented at a CSIS conference 'Prospects for improving US–China–Africa relations', http://www.chathamhouse.org/sites/default/files/public/Research/Africa/angolachina_csis.pdf, accessed 17 April 2012

Corkin, L. (2008) 'All's fair in loans and war: the development of China–Angola relations', in K. Ampiah, and S. Naidu (eds) *Crouching Tiger*,

Hidden Dragon? African and China, Scottsville, KY, University of KwaZulu-Natal Press

Hongmei, L. and Tang, L. (2009) 'Corporate social responsibility communication of Chinese and global corporations in China', http://phbs.edu.cn/info/UserFiles/2009-12/18/20091218173516962.pdf, accessed 15 August 2011

Jornal de Angola (2009) 'Comércio Angola–China superaos 25 mil milhões' [Angola–China trade exceeds 25 thousand million], May

Jornal de Angola (2011) Interview with Chinese ambassador in Angola, Zhang Bolun, 21 March

Macauhub (2009) 'Chinese companies in Angola create a chamber of commerce', www.macauhub.com.mo, accessed 15 August 2011

Ministry of Finance, Republic of Angola (2008a) Technical Support Bureau, Line of Credit/Eximbank of China, 'Relatório das actividades desenvolvidas I trimestre' [Report of activities developed in the first quarter]

Ministry of Finance, Republic of Angola (2008b) Technical Support Bureau, Line of Credit/Eximbank of China, 'Relatório das actividades desenvolvidas II trimestre' [Report of activities developed in the second quarter]

Ministry of Finance, Republic of Angola (2008c) Technical Support Bureau, Line of Credit/Eximbank of China, 'Projectos concluídos' [Completed projects], June

Ministry of Foreign Relations, Republic of Angola (2009) 'Memorando sobre as relações de cooperação entre a República de Angola e a República da China' [Memoranda on cooperation relations between the Republic of Angola and the Republic of China], May

Novo Jornal (2011) 25 March: 11

Vines, A., Wong, L., Weimer, M. and Campos, I. (2009) *Thirst for African Oil: Asian National Oil Companies in Nigeria and Angola*, London, Chatham House

9

The untold story of Chinese perceptions of Angola

Liu Haifang

Introduction

The China–Angola relationship has become an extremely topical subject worldwide since 2004 when the two countries signed a multi-billion dollar loan agreement.[1] Campos and Vines discuss the idea of China and Angola's special relationship constituting 'a perfect marriage' and examine the idea that Sino-Angolan cooperation has been beneficial to both sides.[2] Indeed, the impact of this cooperation on Angola's post-war reconstruction has been investigated by many scholars with a significant emphasis on the relevant merits of the 'Angola mode' of Chinese lending. In one recently published paper, an Angolan scholar noted that the Angola mode was 'an innovative model that embodies China's notion of win-win cooperation, where an oil-backed credit line is used to finance the reconstruction and development of infrastructure.'[3] Yet, quoting Nyerere's famous words about 'unequal equals', this 'pragmatic partnership'[4] has been defined as an asymmetrical bilateral relation.[5] Later, this relationship has been described as having gone sour for a period, only to be repaired further down the line because of the worldwide financial crisis, given Angola's heavy reliance on Chinese money to fund its large-scale national reconstruction and development.[6] For some observers though, China and Angola will continue to make 'uneasy allies' for some time into the foreseeable future.[7]

Studies of Sino-Angolan relations have typically been focused on macro-level economic cooperation, be it on construction, oil or the finance sector, while the medium or micro-level social dimensions have been neglected. How society and individuals from both sides have actively participated in the process remains a neglected theme so far in much of the established literature, as does the study of underlying perceptions and motivations (particularly in China). The difficulties in carrying out this kind of study are considerable, due in part to the high cost of living in Angola, the language and cultural barriers for researchers, and the reticence of the officials on both sides.[8]

This chapter seeks to fill in this gap from the Chinese side and is based in part on participatory observations and interviews the author made in her two trips to Angola but also on a variety of literature on Angola or Sino-Angola relations written in Chinese[9] including newspapers, popular journals, academic journals, blogs and popular websites. The chapter will thus analyse Chinese public opinion towards Angola and the changing nature of bilateral relations from 1975 until the present, in order to understand the evolution of Chinese perceptions of Angola and what has motivated so many Chinese citizens to go to Angola in search of their fortune.

Theories and methods

In short, this is a cultural study that seeks to investigate the social forces at work in the process of history making, the objective of which is to determine how, since the early 1980s, a variety of media and different forms of cultural expression have encouraged the Chinese public to have a passion for Angola and to consider travelling or migrating to the country. From then on, as Chinese society was experiencing the rapid process of reform, the opening of doors and marketisation, 'culture' has grown out of the traditional arena (where it was considered to be the sum of arts and knowledge) to enter the domains of institutions and everyday life. Thus, as Raymond Williams has argued, we need to have a cultural theory so that we can understand the diversified dimensions of the whole historical process and the real social trends that hide beneath the surface of everyday life.[10] In the discipline of international relations this kind of analysis tends to be understood as constructionist theory. This chapter seeks to use this method to examine the role of public knowledge and interests, as social forces, in shaping the international relations between these two 'partners'.

Periodisation of the history of Sino-Angolan relations

Conventional periodisations of the history of Sino-Angolan relations often regard 2002 as the watershed, assuming that the Chinese are risk averse and therefore only started to enter into Angola in large numbers after the long civil war.[11] This is quite a limited view, however, which suggests that Chinese companies, individual businessmen and entrepreneurs were waiting at the starting line in 2002[12] and then rushed into Angola overnight ahead of their peers from any other countries. Instead this chapter goes back to 1975, the time Angola gained independence, to get a better understanding of the historical context. Table 9.1 details the numbers of relevant items of Chinese literature on Angola for each decade since the 1970s, drawn from a variety of databases.

Clearly, in terms of numbers, there is an obvious increasing trend, but the trend started from the mid-1980s onward, although a dramatic increase did indeed take place at the end of the war in 2002. The obvious reason could be the establishment of bilateral diplomatic relations, yet an analysis of other data sources can help to develop our understanding of this even further.

Table 9.1 Numbers of relevant items of literature on Angola from various databases

Sources of the literature	1975–85	1986–95	1996–2002	2003– January 2011
National journals database (from 1979)	78	185	197	648
PhD thesis database (from 1999)	–	–	0	1
Excellent MA thesis database (from 1999)	–	–	2	16
Important meetings database (from 2000)	–	–	0	8
Important newspaper database (from 2000)	–	–	29	280
Totals	78	185	228	953

Table 9.2 Numbers of relevant items of literature on Angola according to subject

	1975–85	1986–95	1996–2002	2003–January 2011	Trend from percentage
Politics	67	151	95	71	↓
Economic system and its reform	8	15	17	72	↓
Agro economy	5	9	12	0	↓
Light manufacturing	4	27	22	0	↓
Biography	2	0	5	0	↓
Trade	–	108	23	136	↑↑
Petrol and oil	–	–	20	166	↑↑
Investment	–	–	7	187	↑↑↑
Finance	–	–	–	186	↑↑↑
Securities	–	–	–	174	↑↑↑
Architecture & engineering	–	–	–	93	↑↑
Physical education	–	–	–	60	↑↑
Macroeconomic management & sustainable development	–	–	–	39	↑↑
Road & waterway transportation	–	–	–	34	↑↑
Market analysis & information	–	–	–	30	↑↑

Note: An item of literature can cover more than one subject.

The transformation of interest by decade

Specifically, in each period of time, the numbers of available items of literature can also be broken down accordingly into specific themes and subjects:

Politics reigned

In the first stage, 1975–85, a significant number of these literatures were concerned with politics. Most of these were reports and commentaries about the Angolan civil war yet, interestingly enough, how South Africa, Cuba, the Soviet Union and the US were involved. How the war impacted upon the liberation process of southern Africa as a whole (especially Namibia) was a key feature of much of this work while the three competing liberation movements in Angola were hardly in focus at all.[13] This of course reflects the reality that China did not have a diplomatic relationship yet with Angola and the priority of the Chinese government's strategy in Africa was to support anti-colonial liberation, yet somehow it was very much affected by the ideological debate with the Soviet Union.

Angola agencies and interaction at the grassroots

In the second stage, 1986–95, since the formal diplomatic relationship had already been established, literature reporting on the status of Angola's war, the difficult peace process and the various meetings and negotiations on Angola's future became the most important topics. Along with some reports on the social situation in Angola (regarding issues such as how people's lives had been affected by landmines and malaria),[14] reports and analysis on Angola's economy and economic reform became another priority. Angola's agricultural development and its international economic cooperation was another key focus attracting attention, including work on the river and fishery development with Namibia and also oil extraction.[15] One very interesting short report in 1986 concerned Angola's cooperation with Brazil around dam construction including a discussion of how Angola paid off the loan with oil.[16] This is, of course, exactly the same kind of deal that we hear so much about today in references to the 'Angola mode' that the Angolan government developed in its relations with China, which has been interpreted by various publications as either a conventional type of agreement typical in the history of the extraction sector[17] or an invention that China developed from its own experience of aid assistance in dealing with Japanese loans.[18]

The diversity of interests was partly a product of the rapid development of bilateral relations after normalisation in 1983. Agricultural cooperation had made some progress (e.g. in the dry rice aid project that the Chinese government provided)[19] but scholastic interests were also beginning to emerge amongst Chinese Africanists and some historical and artistic studies were also published in this period.[20]

An article from *Voice of Friendship* recorded the trip of a delegation of Angolan youth entrepreneurs to China, which provides strong evidence of the bilateral economic relations that were beginning to develop in the 1980s and 1990s and helps to counter and demystify the idea of the Chinese community suddenly 'swarming' into Angola only after the end of the war in 2002. According to this report, the Angolan entrepreneurs came in 1994, when lots of Chinese products were already very popular in the Angola market, though 80 per cent were imported from other countries. The delegation was motivated by the popularity of Chinese goods and they came partly to identify the reason behind this.[21] The delegation did not accept the Chinese organisers' plan for them to purely visit tourist resorts, instead insisting on meeting and interacting with Chinese entrepreneurs, with some even deciding to establish some joint ventures cooperatively with Chinese counterparts. According to the report, this successful visit was mainly attributable to the historical link between Chinese and Angolan people. The head of the delegation was also the son of a linguistic expert who spent six years in China in the 1960s together with his son. Some 20 years after he returned to Angola the son decided to dedicate his life to promoting people-to-people relations and to reviving his capacity for speaking Chinese.

One article, written by the former Chinese ambassador to Angola and published in 1999, vividly recounts the most challenging experiences of Chinese diplomats during the failed peace negotiations and after the unsuccessful national elections in 1992.[22] Besides diplomats and over 30 Chinese businessmen, there were, according to the ambassador, some 380 Chinese people working on contract services in Angola at that time. This would seem to provide further evidence that there were emerging grassroots-level relations and interactions from the 1980s until the beginning of 1990s and before the civil war of the 1990s forced most businessmen to retreat to China.

Business interest rising

The third stage, 1996–2002, is most meaningful for this study. Politically, this period of time saw the most violent part of the civil war between MPLA and UNITA, which understandably is reflected strongly in Chinese literature. At the same time, the representation of Angola in Chinese literature started to become more multi-faceted with articles concerned with bilateral relations at the peak of the war or commenting on and remembering particular political figures such as the leader of UNITA, Jonas Savimbi, or Viriato Da Cruz, the poet and ex-leader of the MPLA, who spent his final days in China and died there.[23] As early as the 1960s, there were a range of publications on Angola that were translated into Chinese, such as poetry anthologies of António Agostinho Neto, or the basic constitution of MPLA. This kind of diversified interest in Angola started to re-emerge again in China in the 1990s; it helped to rekindle popular interest in the country and also began to connect with the increasing desire for engaging with more external markets that was coming from China's business elites.

Compared with the literatures on politics, a more obvious trend is the rising interest in business and trade information, ranging from literature on the general business climate and regulations and a new tax tariff towards foreign companies, to oil field information (since new Angolan oil fields required operators), energy, power and other sectors which were expected to rejuvenate.[24]

Together with this kind of very practical and useful information for doing business, there was also lots of very appealing news about the attractiveness of Angola's market, including a report regarding the potential trend towards Angola becoming the biggest oil producer in Africa.[25] A journalist from *People's Daily*, taking advantage of the end of the long-lasting war, even wrote an encouraging piece with the heading: 'The opportunities of Angola market should not be missed'.[26]

According to one businessman who went to Angola in 1999 there were just 22 Chinese nationals (including diplomats) in Angola at that time.[27] This period, however, saw more bilateral official visits, especially from the Angolan side, including President dos Santos's second visit to China in 1998, the visit of the MPLA general secretary in 2000 and the visit of the parliament speaker in 2001. These were all reported in the Chinese media, particularly dos Santos's three-day visit to Guangdong province and to the most rapidly developing city, Shenzhen. During dos Santos's trip to China, the intentional loan agreement initiated in 1984 (for the purpose of constructing economic houses in Viana District) was finalised, together with another set of bilateral agreements, including the RMB 5 million grant from the Chinese government and an agreement on cultural and educational cooperation.[28] This is also evidence that there had been a concessional loan arrangement between Angola and China before 2004 when the $2 billion credit line was signed. Neither was the building of economic houses for the Angolan government a new experience for Chinese companies in 2004 as it had started in the 1990s. According to a journalist from the *People's Daily* writing in 1999, Chinese construction companies had earned their own 'fame' in the Angolan market.[29]

There were also several reports concerned with the relations between specific Chinese and Angolan individuals. For example, Angola's first lady visited China in 1996 where she went to the Shanghai Children's Welfare House and donated some money as a token of her love for children with disabilities.[30] From the Chinese side, a woman delegate also visited Angola in 1999 and the *Journal of China's Woman* subsequently published an essay which listed the issues Angolan women were encountering, such as polygamy.[31]

Civil society speaks

The fourth stage, 2002 to the present day, provides a rich and interesting insight into the changing dynamics of Chinese perceptions of Angola and of the deepening bilateral relations between the two countries. On the one hand, many new areas began to be explored in the available literatures and the overall volume of literature increased significantly; on the other hand, the issues being discussed were beginning to be explored in a more in-depth and practical way, as in the case, for example, of one article about the Luanda port published through a popular journal – the first piece of Chinese literature to analyse the port systematically using first-hand, primary data.[32] Consequently, as bilateral economic cooperation was intensifying and investment, trade and oil were rapidly attracting ever-increasing attention, political topics were no longer the primary focus of much of this work. Based on personal or collective experiences of different economic areas in Angola, many Chinese people authored professional papers, reflecting upon the nature of bilateral cooperation and of the Angolan economic environment with a view to the development of long-term investment strategies and drawing out the lessons for Chinese entrepreneurs' further overseas development.

Since most Chinese companies in Angola started in the construction industry, through their involvement in basic post-war infrastructure reconstruction and civil engineering and renovation, they were enabled to become more competitive, which in turn enabled the Chinese to develop a sustainable presence in the Angolan market. In 2007, a postgraduate student of Chongqing University, who worked in a Chinese construction company in Angola right from the beginning of its involvement in the country, published an academic paper on risk management in construction.[33] At the same time, and based on his work experience in the Chinese company, he even wrote a master's thesis reflecting upon the Chinese construction company's growing experience and the potential risks it was exposed to in Angola.[34] According to the author, there could be many risks ahead which Chinese construction companies were not yet fully aware of and which were in large part attributable to the legacies of Angola's economic planning system.[35] All the lessons and suggestions discussed in Li's two essays are very practical and would have been considered very useful for other construction companies seeking to develop a presence in the Angolan market.

Similarly, some Chinese people who had been involved in Angola's railway rehabilitation projects (such as the Benguela railway rehabilitation carried out by Chinese Railway Group,

CR-20) published some papers regarding the differences between Angolan narrow gauge railways and the features of other Chinese and Angolan railway transportation systems and discussed possible options for the renovation of the famous Tan-Zam railway that connects the eastern and western coasts of the African continent.[36] Likewise, people participating in the project of rehabilitating the water supply system in Luanda, or other municipal engineering projects, also published papers recounting their working experiences (and the differences from their previous experiences in China) and raised new suggestions both for the projects in Angola and for the development of Chinese companies' developments abroad, including suggestions on how to manage local workers.[37] Through a journal entitled *Hongshui River* (named after the famous river in Guangxi province), over ten people from the Guangxi Hydroelectric Construction Bureau published articles on themes including overseas project management, water supply engineering, sustainable development, cost management and oil-supply management.[38]

Unsurprisingly, therefore, since 2003 there has been a significant volume of literature published concerning Angolan oil and Sino-Angolan energy cooperation. This not only reports on new events and developments, but also includes scientific papers analyzing the strengths and shortcomings of energy cooperation and how to avoid issues such as legal risks.[39] Naturally, papers on risks in this cooperation area are amongst the most widely circulated as is evident from the high frequency of downloads from the Chinese National Knowledge Infrastructure.

The investment and finance sectors have seemingly drawn the most attention since 2003, yet interestingly most debates and discussions on securities and finances related to Angola that appeared both through printed publications and on the internet, have only documented one listed Chinese company, Hangxiao – this is a big player in infrastructure projects in Angola and was also involved in a high profile insider trading case in China. This topic of insider trading in China has little to do with understanding the Angolan finance sector but is often used as a window onto the nature of Chinese dealings with Angola. Yet arguably this case is better used to illustrate the monitoring efforts coming from within China's own rising civil society and the increasing importance of communication technologies. The storm surrounding this company lasted more than a year from March 2007 when the price of its stock suddenly doubled. Four years after this, printed literature and internet articles about Hangxiao companies and the Chinese International Fund (CIF) (which is registered in Hong Kong and which was regarded as the wayfinder to the Angolan market for many Chinese companies) still continued to appear from time to time, though few could offer convincing explanations of why this had happened and one wonders whether such a big order for a construction project in Angola ever existed in the first place.[40]

Also evident during this period of time is a range of articles concerned with Angola and bilateral relations published in popular journals, including one article reflecting upon China's transformative role from the time of Angola's liberation and civil war to the contemporary notion of China as a peacebuilder.[41] On the one hand, it shows the rising interest among ordinary Chinese people in China's international role; on the other hand, it also illustrates the rising interest in Angola following its emergence as the biggest oil supplier to China in 2005. Similarly, the Chinese media started to pay attention to, and to reprint articles from, the foreign media about both Angola and bilateral relations.[42] Of course, one of the reasons behind this is that the Chinese media still lacks the capacity to observe Angola directly.

Important findings

As Chinese society started to change quite rapidly in the early 1980s, so too have Chinese perceptions towards Angola begun to shift. In the Chinese literature published before diplomatic relations were established, Angola was seen as little more than a field of competition for the US and allies of the Soviet Union and Cuba. Since the middle of the 1980s, however, Angola has suddenly became much more meaningful in Chinese literature with one scholar even researching the origins of geographic names in the country.[43] A real diversity of interests started to appear in the 1990s when Chinese products required overseas markets, and Angolan labour contracts and oil extraction began to look quite promising to the Chinese. As the established literatures demonstrated, at this stage, large parts were dedicated to introducing all sectors of the Angolan market to the Chinese. Consequently, there were some Chinese contract labourers and businessmen in Angola, and the grassroots level interaction was developing well even though the 1992 war restricted this trend. Much of this everyday, grassroots interaction, however, has been overlooked in the current studies of Sino-Angolan relations.

Indeed, Chinese perceptions towards Angola and the relationship between the countries have made significant progress since 2002, partly due to the growth of bilateral cooperation and the rapid development of information technologies. In this period several cases show that civil society has consciously been getting involved in observing these bilateral relations. Knowledge of Angola increased markedly through the publication of several professional papers by Chinese individuals, many of whom had previously worked as practitioners on particular Chinese projects in Angola. However, the dissemination of this work amongst ordinary Chinese people is quite limited and the influence this knowledge has had on recent Chinese investors in the Angolan market is still unclear. Horizontal communications are not common among Chinese practitioners in Angola, as I have found in my two previous field visits to Angola, and whether culture is a factor in this, or it is completely attributable to the ways in which Chinese companies operate, warrants further study, perhaps through the use of in-depth interviews.

In the first 20 years after independence, official relations and governmental policies determined how much ordinary people could know about Angola and the nature of bilateral relations; but after the 1990s, as society itself was awakening in China, ordinary Chinese people started to contribute to the history-making process themselves, partly as a consequence of the growing hunger for knowledge about the Angolan market. As both the interviews and my analysis of blogs illustrates,[44] most Chinese traders were motivated by a strong passion for seeking their fortunes in Angola, with or without knowing the risks involved in the ongoing war. Some even came to Angola in the 1990s when bullets were still flying. Without enough capital to engage in the alloy business (which could be up to 30 times more profitable in Angola) as word of mouth had recommended, most started to engage and invest in fast moving consumer goods and then turned to invest in manufacturing or construction materials that were highly sought after in Angola. Without the bravery of these pioneers, the multi-billion dollar deal between China and Angola may not have happened in 2002 and Chinese knowledge about Angola might be still very limited.

As Hangxiao's case demonstrates, the monitoring conducted by civil society organisations in China has become an increasingly important influence on the behaviour of Chinese companies. At the same time, however, civil society monitoring remains quite small scale and the accumulation of public knowledge is still rather limited in some areas. For example, there is a significant amount of literature on stock markets that occasionally include the word 'Angola' but none have seriously asked or talked about Angola's own stock market yet. There is still very little literature on Angolan arts, culture, sciences and social development.

Conclusion

The purpose of this paper was to investigate the social forces in history making, regarding the accumulation in China of public knowledge on Angola and the changing nature of bilateral relations between the two countries. Transcending the data on the number and value of loans that the Chinese have provided to Angola, this chapter has sought to produce a more human face to the story of the evolution of bilateral relations. First, contrary to the conventional perspective on bilateral relations that suggests they were built suddenly and only after the end of the war in 2002, this chapter has sought to document some of intensive exchanges (especially at the grassroots level) that existed in the late 1980s and 1990s and upon which the closer cooperation since 2002 has been able to build. Secondly, societal interests have been shaping and also limiting Chinese public knowledge on Angola, and therefore the overall pattern of bilateral relations. Obviously an effort to uncover more elements of this developing relationship and to incorporate them into Chinese public knowledge is required, including attention to Angola's rich society and culture, and this enriched public knowledge could assist in shaping future bilateral relations in a more balanced way.

Notes

1. See publications in notes 2–7. Also Alves, A.C. (2010) 'The Oil factor in Sino-Angolan relations at the start of the 21st century', *SAIIA Occasional Paper*, 55.
2. Campos, I. and Vines, A. (2008) 'Angola and China: a pragmatic partnership', Working paper presented at a CSIS conference 'Prospects for improving US–China–Africa relations', http://www.chathamhouse. org/sites/default/files/public/Research/Africa/angolachina_csis.pdf, accessed 17 April 2012
3. Kiala, C. (2010) 'China–Angola aid relations: strategic cooperation for development?', *South African Journal of International Affairs*, 17(3): 313–31.
4. Dos Santos's words, referred to in Campos and Vines (2008).
5. Campbell, H. and Chaulia, S. (2009) 'Unequal equals: Angola and China', *World Affairs*, 13(1): 44–83.
6. Vines, A., Wong, L., Weimer, M. and Campos, I. (2009) *Thirst for African Oil: Asian National Oil Companies in Nigeria and Angola*, London, Chatham House.
7. Corkin, L. (2011) 'Uneasy allies: China's evolving relations with Angola', *Journal of Contemporary African Studies*, 29(2): 169–80.
8. Campos and Vines (2008), see note 2.
9. Some of these have been digitalised and could be read through electronic devices. However, some in printed form are not yet accessible in libraries.
10. Williams, R. (1961) *The Long Revolution*, London, Chatto & Windus: 41; Williams, R. (1958) *Culture and Society 1780–1950*, London, Penguin.
11. See for example 'The oil factor in Sino-Angolan relations at the start of the 21st century' (2010), *SAIIA Occasional Paper*, 55. The author thinks there have been three distinct phases in Sino–Angolan bilateral relations: (1) prior to the establishment of diplomatic ties (1975–83), (2) between then and the end of the civil war (1983–2002), and (3) from then onwards (2002 to the present).
12. Of course, for any study on Angola, 2002 is unavoidably a key watershed.
13. e.g. Zan Wei, C. (1978) 'Why is the north polar bear leaping into Africa', *World Affairs*, 1, January; Zan Wei, C. (1982) 'A new round of fights over Southern Africa', *World Affairs*, 8, April; Wu Shi (1983) 'The contest in Southern Africa between Soviet Union and USA', *Journal of International Studies*, May; Zan Wei, C. (1982) 'How South Africa invaded Angola', *World Affairs*, 6, September; Xing Long (1982) 'Soviet Union–Cuba allies in Africa', *Digest of Contemporary Foreign Social Sciences*.
14. Hailiang, W. (1994) 'Devil's seeds: landmines', *World Affairs*, 6, March; Zhiliang, S. (1986) 'There are malaria cases anti-existing medicines in Angola', *Foreign Medication*, 2.
15. e.g. Ou Ge (1988) 'Why has the dry rice experiment succeeded in Angola', *International Economic Cooperation*, March; Jianping, N. (1991) 'Angola and Namibia cooperate to develop river on borders', *Water Conservancy and Hydroelectric Technologies*, May; Xingyu, Z. (1987) 'The Angolan economy full of difficulties', *West Asian and African Studies*, October; Yong, W.

(1995) 'Angola is busy with building offshore infrastructure for oil extraction', *China Offshore Platform*, 1.

16. Zhuxun, D. (1985) 'Brazil accepted oil as compensation to build dam for Angola', *People's Yangzi River*, 1 May.
17. Foster, V., Butterfield, W., Chen, C. and Pushak, N. (2009) 'Building bridges: China's growing role as infrastructure financier for sub-Saharan Africa', Washington DC, The World Bank.
18. Brautigam, D. (2009) *The Dragon's Gift: The Real Story of China in Africa*, Oxford, Oxford University Press.
19. Ou Ge (1988), see note 15.
20. e.g. Dong Bo (2007) 'On the impacts of forced labour system enforced by Portugal in Angola and Mozambique', *West Asian and African Studies*, October; Zhiwei, Y. (1993) 'Building Angola's pre-historic art data bank', *Quaternary Sciences*, October: 258–66.
21. Shulin, L. (1994) 'Report of Angolan entrepreneurs in China', *Voices of Friendship*, 5.
22. Baosheng, Z. (1999) 'Diplomatic relation is a special battle line: days to stay and take care of Chinese embassy in Angola during the war', *World Affairs*, 16 (August).
23. Huang Ci (2002) 'From liberator to terrorist: how Savimbi died', *Nan feng Chuang* (Window of Southern Wind), 6 (March); Baosheng (1996) see note 22; Bingzhen, W. (1996) 'An Angolan poet staying in China', *World Affairs*, 10 (May).
24. He Yulan, Song Peijin and Song Quigen (1997) 'Evaluation on Angolan Palanca crude oil and discussion on the processing scheme', *Guang Zhou Chemical Industry and Technology*, 1; *International Market for Machinery and Electronics* (1995) 'Angola updates tax tariff', April 1995; *Northern China Electricity Section* (1999) 'Angola is opening its electric power market' (11); *International Market for Machinery and Electronics* (1995) 'Angola enforces new business inspection regulations', April.
25. Yue, C. (2000) 'Angola might become the biggest oil producer in Africa', *Newspaper of China's Petroleum*, November 16.
26. Huang Zequan (2002) 'Golden opportunities to explore markets in Angola', *International Economic Cooperation*, 8: 51–54.
27. Interview with Xu Ning, president of China–Angolan Business Council, 10 March 2009, Luanda, Angola.
28. Website of Angolan embassy in China: 'The cooperation between Angola and China', http://www.angolaembassy-china.com/coperacaocn.html, accessed 24 January 2011.
29. Fu Xiancheng (2000) 'Chinese construction companies have made their fame in Angola market', *Hebei Economic Daily*, 30 November.
30. Qiyun, S. (1996) 'Give love to children: first lady of Angola visits Shanghai children welfare house', *Voices of Friendship*, 4.
31. Ge, B. (2001) 'Impressions of Lesotho and Angola', *Journal of China's Woman*, 3.
32. Yong, Z. (2010) 'On West African Port Luanda', *Marine Technology*, 1.

33. Dongming, L. and Shirong, L. (2007) 'Risk management for the Angola project: analysis and suggestions', *Journal of Chongqing Jiaotong University* (Social Sciences Edition), S1.
34. Dongming, L. (2007) 'Strategic analyses of a Chinese construction corporation in growing period in Angola', master's degree thesis of Chongqing University.
35. Ibid.
36. Huli, Q. (2010) (CR Group20), 'A probe into the mechanic pavement of narrow gauge railways', *Nation Defense, Transportation Engineering and Technologies*, 9; Jian, Y. (2010) (CR Shanghai Planning Academy Group), 'On Angolan Benguela railway's transportation organizing model', *Railway Transportation and Economy*, December; Jian, G. (2010) (CR Shanghai Planning Academy Group), 'Discussion on different options of Benguela railway's reconstruction', *Railway Transportation and Economy*, July.
37. Yingbang, L. and Rongmei, W. (2009) 'In the Angolan electricity market, how to manage local workers', *Guangxi Electricity*, 30 September.
38. Haoxin, Z. (2010) 'Cost management in the Angola market', *Hongshui River*, August; Feng, L. (2010) 'Pay attention to oil supply for the sake of oil supply security in the Angola project', *Hongshui River*, August; Haoxin, Z. and Pingyu, Z. (2010) 'Skills and strategies in the process of bidding in the Angola Market', *Hongshui River*, August; Jinhe,W. (2010) 'Material management in the Angola project', *Hongshui River*, August, etc.
39. *China Chemical Reporter* (2009) 'CNOOC and Sinopec to buy Angola stake', 6 August; Xiao, L. (2011) 'Remote and near concerns for Chinese oil interests in Africa under the circumstance of the American Hegemony', *Hu Nan Social Sciences*, November; Wei, W. (2011) 'Measures African oil countries are taking to attract investment', *Foreign Economic and Trade Affairs*, November; Fei, X. (2006) 'Chinese enterprises' steps in Angola: oil makes bridge', *Nanfeng Chuang*, 6; Xingwang, Q., Demin, C. and Guangbing, Z. (2009) 'On international legal guarantee towards Sino-Angolan oil cooperation', *International Business*, June; Sheng, K. (2010) 'Risks and measures to counter risks in the Sino-Angolan energy cooperation', *West Asia and Africa*, 1.
40. The volume of literature on this Hangxiao case is huge. Just to list several examples: Fu, Z (2007) 'The real poisonous cancer of Hangxiao Case', *Chinese Entrepreneurs*, May; Yaqin, S. (2008) 'Difficult to unravel: the devil stock of Hangxiao', *Security Daily*, September; Zhenhua, Z. (2010) 'The shocking insider trade', *Financial Economy*, November; Jinlin, S. (2010) 'After removal of the big order, Hangxiao tests water with its investment in real estate in Angola', *Security Daily*, February.
41. Jing, L. (2006) 'China's image in the flame of war of Africa: Angola as a case', *Nanfeng Chuang*, 116.
42. Such as 'American media says, the love affairs between China and Angola is cooling', *Global Times*, http://china.huanqiu.com/eyes_on_china/economy/2010-08/1010364.html, accessed 5 March 2012. This news was immediately copied again and again through the internet.

43. Shishun, S. (1983) 'Origins of the geographic names of Angola and the changes', *West Asia and Africa*, 5.
44. Such as 'Africablog' (http://www.africawindows.com/site/html/85/6185-257.html), 'angolaproject blog' (http://blog.sina.com.cn/angolaproject) and the 'Angola post bar', on the bulletin board of Baidu, the most popular search engine among the mainland Chinese netizens (http://tieba.baidu.com/p/355339291).

Index

Chinese and African Perspectives on China in Africa

Edited by Axel Harneit-Sievers, Stephen Marks and Sanusha Naidu

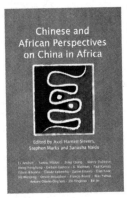

2010
paperback
978-1-906387-33-4
also available in pdf, epub
and Kindle formats

The deepening engagement of China in Africa has led to debates about the evolving nature of this relationship. Yet the analysis has largely focused on interactions between states, with little attention on the growing dialogue between Chinese and African civil society organisations. These essays, written by African and Chinese scholars and activists, explore the interaction between non-state actors and argue that the future of Africa–China relations rests on including such voices.

This book assesses patterns of investment, legal cooperation, effects on the environment, trade, aid and labour links, questions of peace, security and stability, the African Union response, possible regulatory interventions and the future strengthening of the dialogue between Chinese and African civil society organisations.

'Well written and very thoughtful ... This book is an excellent read for students and scholars of political science, international relations and international political economy.'

Richard B. Dadzie, *African Affairs*

Order your copy from www.pambazukapress.org

China's New Role in Africa and the South

Edited by Dorothy Guerrero and Firoze Manji

China's global expansion is usually talked about from the viewpoint of the West. These essays, by scholars and activists from China and the global South, provide diverse views on the challenges faced by Africa, Latin America and Asia as a result of China's rise as a global economic power. Chinese aid, trade and investments – driven by the needs of its own economy – present both threats and opportunities for the South, requiring an analysis that goes beyond simplistic caricatures of 'good' and 'evil'.

2008
paperback
978-1-906387-26-6
also available in pdf, epub
and Kindle formats

'... important new perspectives on this emerging issue within international relations.'

**Johanna Jansson, *The China Monitor*,
Centre for Chinese Studies, Stellenbosch University**

India in Africa: Changing Geographies of Power

Edited by Emma Mawdsley and Gerard McCann

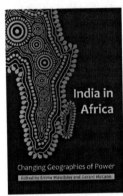

India in Africa

Changing Geographies of Power

Edited by Emma Mawdsley and Gerard McCann

2011
paperback
978-1-906387-65-5
also available in pdf, epub
and Kindle formats

Major changes are taking place in the global economy and polity. While China's relationship to Africa is much examined, knowledge and analysis of India's role in Africa has until now been limited but, as a significant global player, India's growing interactions with various African countries call for detailed analysis of the Asian giant's influence and its relations with the continent.

In this original book, which enables readers to compare India to China and other 'rising powers' in Africa, expert African, Indian and western commentators draw on a collection of accessibly written case studies to explore inter-related areas, including trade, investment, development aid, civil society relations, security and geopolitics.

'An indispensable book for those who want to understand the compulsion and politics of recent Chinese and Indian involvement in Africa, written by experts in a language accessible to the non-expert.'

Yash Ghai, activist, and scholar of international law, and chairman of the Constitution of Kenya Review Commission 2000-2004

'A book that must be read by anyone seeking to understand the contextual change affecting India-Africa relations: the transition from political solidarities of the past, to new relations based on commercial imperatives.'

Davinder Lamba, executive director of the Mazingira Institute, Nairobi

 Order your copy from www.pambazukapress.org

African Perspectives on China in Africa

Edited by Firoze Manji and Stephen Marks

China's involvement in Africa has provoked much discussion. Is China just the latest exploiter, putting its own economic interests above environmental or human rights concerns? Or is China's engagement an extension of 'South–South solidarity'? Does China's involvement enable African countries to free themselves from debt and conditionality? Or is Africa swapping one tyranny for another? Lost in the discussion have been the voices of African analysts and activists. They are heard in these essays, demonstrating that there is no single 'African view' about China in Africa.

2007
paperback
978-0-9545637-3-8
also available in pdf, epub
and Kindle formats

'This book is an interesting and easy read, granting the reader access to an enriching debate and opening new questions.'

Tania Adam, Centre d'Estudis Africans, Barcelona